Information Security and Cryptography
Texts and Monographs

T0181319

For further volumes:
http://www.springer.com/series/4752

Sergey Yekhanin

Locally Decodable Codes and Private Information Retrieval Schemes

 Springer

Dr. Sergey Yekhanin
Microsoft Research
Silicon Valley Lab
La Avenida 1065
Mountain View, CA 94043
USA
yekhanin@microsoft.com

Series Editors
Prof. Dr. David Basin
Prof. Dr. Ueli Maurer
ETH Zürich
Switzerland
basin@inf.ethz.ch
maurer@inf.ethz.ch

ISSN 1619-7100
ISBN 978-3-642-26577-8   ISBN 978-3-642-14358-8 (eBook)
DOI 10.1007/978-3-642-14358-8
Springer Heidelberg Dordrecht London New York

ACM Computing Classification (1998): E.4

Cover design: KuenkelLopka GmbH, Heidelberg

Printed on acid-free paper

Springer is part of Springer Science+Business Media (www.springer.com)

To my sister Yulia

Preface

This book studies two closely related notions, namely locally decodable codes (LDCs) and private information retrieval (PIR) schemes.

Locally decodable codes are a class of error-correcting codes. Error-correcting codes help ensure reliable transmission of information over noisy channels, as well as reliable storage of information on a medium that may become partially corrupted over time or whose reading device is subject to errors. Such codes allow one to add redundancy, or bit strings, to messages, encoding them into longer bit strings, called codewords, in such a way that the message can still be recovered even if a certain fraction of the codeword bits are corrupted. In typical applications of error-correcting codes the message is first partitioned into small blocks, each of which is then encoded separately. This encoding strategy allows efficient random-access retrieval of the information, since one needs to decode only the portion of data in which one is interested. Unfortunately, this strategy yields poor noise resilience, since when even a single block (out of possibly tens of thousands) is completely corrupted, some information is lost. In view of this limitation, it would seem preferable to encode the whole message into a single codeword of an error-correcting code. Such a solution improves the robustness to noise but is hardly satisfactory, since one needs to look at the whole codeword in order to recover any particular bit of the message (at least when using classical error-correcting codes). Such decoding complexity is prohibitive for today's massive data sets.

Locally decodable codes are codes that simultaneously provide efficient random-access retrieval and high noise resilience by allowing reliable reconstruction of an arbitrary bit of the message from looking at only a small number of randomly chosen codeword bits. Local decodability comes at the price of a certain loss in terms of code efficiency. Specifically, locally decodable codes require longer codeword lengths than their classical counterparts.

Private information retrieval schemes are cryptographic protocols designed to safeguard the privacy of database users. They allow clients to retrieve records from public databases while completely hiding the identity of the retrieved records from the database owners. The possibility of retrieving database records without revealing their identities to the owner of the database may seem beyond hope. Note, however, that a trivial solution is available: when users want a single record, they can ask for a copy of the whole database. This solution involves enormous communication overhead, however, and is likely to be unacceptable. It turns out that for users who want to keep their privacy fully protected (in the "information-theoretic" sense), this trivial solution is optimal.

Fortunately, this negative result applies only to databases stored on a single server, and not to databases replicated across several servers. In 1995, Chor et al. came up with PIR schemes that enable private retrieval of records from replicated databases, with a nontrivially small amount of communication. In such protocols, users query each server holding the database. The protocol ensures that each individual server (by observing only the query it receives) gets no information about the identity of the items of interest to the user.

In this book, we provide a fresh algebraic look at the theory of locally decodable codes and private information retrieval schemes. We obtain new families of LDCs and PIR schemes that have much better parameters than those of previously known constructions. We also prove some limitations on two server PIR schemes in a restricted setting that covers all currently known schemes.

This version. This book is essentially the same as a dissertation filed with the Massachusetts Institute of Technology in 2007. A few sections and proofs have been expanded to provide more intuition and perspective. In addition, this book has an addendum at the end of every chapter to bring the reader up to date with the various developments in the subjects covered in the book during the period from mid 2007 to mid 2010.

Acknowledgments

I have greatly benefited from Vyacheslav V. Rykov and Arkadii G. D'yachkov, who inspired my interest in mathematics and computer science while I was in high school. I am indebted to them for getting me involved in coding theory research during the first years of my undergraduate studies in Moscow State University and being my well-wishers ever since.

I am greatly indebted to Madhu Sudan, my advisor, for the years of careful nurturing that he provided to me. Madhu's deep intuition and creative approach to technical issues have influenced me a lot. Madhu's highly insightful comments regarding the problems I worked on have been a big factor in aiding my thinking.

While at MIT, I was extremely lucky to meet Swastik Kopparty, my good friend, who provided me with an immense amount of technical expertise in many areas of mathematics.

I am indebted to Kiran Kedlaya, Alexander Razborov, and David Woodruff for collaborations that led to several of the results discussed in this book. I also wish to thank several other people with whom I have had useful discussions on topics related to this thesis. These include Noga Alon, Ilya Dumer, Oded Goldreich, Yuval Ishai, Swastik Kopparty, Igor Pak, Alex Samorodnitsky, Madhu Sudan, Sasha Postnikov, Alex Vardy, and Avi Wigderson.

I would like to thank Cynthia Dwork and all the members of the theory group in the Microsoft Research Silicon Valley Lab – Steve Chien, Frank McSherry, Ilya Mironov, and Kunal Talwar – who hosted me during a fun and productive summer visit in 2006.

The academic environment at MIT was on one hand been very stimulating and on the other it provided me with a wonderful set of friends: Alex Andoni, Elena Grigorescu, MohammadTaghi Hajiaghayi, Nick Harvey, Jon Kelner, Swastik Kopparty, Sayan Mitra, Eddie Nikolova, Mihai Patrascu, Tasos Sidiropoulos, David Woodruff, and Hanson Zhou – thank you!

Contents

Chapter 1
Introduction

This book studies two closely related notions, namely locally decodable codes (LDCs) and private information retrieval (PIR) schemes. Locally decodable codes are error-correcting codes that allow extremely efficient, sublinear-time decoding procedures. Private information retrieval schemes are cryptographic protocols developed in order to protect the privacy of users accessing a public database. We address a long-open question regarding the parameters of optimal LDCs and PIR schemes.

1.1 Locally decodable codes

LDCs are a special kind of error-correcting codes. Error-correcting codes are used to ensure reliable transmission of information over noisy channels and to ensure reliable storage of information on a medium that may become partially corrupted over time (or whose reading device is subject to errors). In both of these applications, the message is typically partitioned into small blocks and then each block is encoded separately. Such an encoding strategy allows efficient random-access retrieval of the information, since one needs to decode only the portion of data one is interested in. Unfortunately, this strategy yields very poor noise resilience, since if even a single block (out of possibly tens of thousands) is completely corrupted, some information is lost. In view of this limitation, it would seem preferable to encode the whole message into a single codeword of an error-correcting code. Such a solution clearly improves the robustness to noise, but is also hardly satisfactory, since one now needs to look at the whole codeword in order to recover any particular bit of the message (at least in the case when classical error-correcting codes are used). Such decoding complexity is prohibitive for modern massive data sets.

Locally decodable codes are error-correcting codes that avoid the problem mentioned above by having extremely efficient *sublinear-time* decoding algorithms. More formally, a k-query locally decodable code C encodes n-bit messages $\mathbf{x}$ in such a way that one can probabilistically recover any bit $\mathbf{x}_i$ of the message by querying only k bits of the (possibly corrupted) codeword $C(\mathbf{x})$, where k can be as small as 2.

S. Yekhanin, *Locally Decodable Codes and Private Information Retrieval Schemes*,
Information Security and Cryptography, DOI 10.1007/978-3-642-14358-8_1,
© Springer-Verlag Berlin Heidelberg 2010

1.1.1 Hadamard code

The classical Hadamard code [65], which encodes n-bit messages to $\exp(n)$-bit codewords[1], provides the simplest nontrivial example of an LDC. In what follows, let $[n]$ denote the set $\{1,\ldots,n\}$. Every coordinate in the Hadamard code corresponds to one subset (out of 2^n) of $[n]$ and stores the XOR of the corresponding bits of the message $\mathbf{x}$. Let $\mathbf{y}$ be an (adversarially corrupted) encoding of $\mathbf{x}$. Given an index $i \in [n]$ and $\mathbf{y}$, the Hadamard decoder picks a set S in $[n]$ uniformly at random and outputs the XOR of the two coordinates of $\mathbf{y}$ corresponding to the sets S and $S \triangle \{i\}$. (Here, $\triangle$ denotes the symmetric difference of sets; for example, $\{1,4,5\} \triangle \{4\} = \{1,5\}$, and $\{1,4,5\} \triangle \{2\} = \{1,2,4,5\}$). It is not difficult to verify that if $\mathbf{y}$ differs from the correct encoding of $\mathbf{x}$ in at most a fraction δ of the coordinates then with probability $1 - 2\delta$ both of the decoder's queries go to uncorrupted locations. In such a case, the decoder correctly recovers the i-th bit of $\mathbf{x}$. The Hadamard code allows a superfast recovery of the message bits (for example, given a codeword corrupted in a fraction 0.1 of the coordinates, one is able to recover any bit of the message with probability 0.8 by reading only two codeword bits).

The main parameters of interest in LDCs are the (codeword) length and the query complexity. The length of the code measures the amount of redundancy that is introduced into a message by the encoder. The query complexity counts the number of bits that need to be read from the (corrupted) codeword in order to recover a single bit of the message. Ideally, one would like to have both of these parameters as small as possible. One cannot, however, minimize the length and the query complexity simultaneously. There is a trade-off. At one end of the spectrum we have classical error-correcting codes [65, 89], which have both a query complexity and a codeword length proportional to the message length. At the other end we have the Hadamard code, which has query complexity 2 and a codeword length exponential in the message length. Establishing the optimal trade-off between the length and the query complexity is the major goal of research in the area of locally decodable codes.

Interestingly, the natural application of locally decodable codes to data transmission and storage described above is neither the historically earliest nor the most important. LDCs have a host of applications in other areas, including cryptography [28, 52], complexity theory [88], and the theory of fault tolerant computation [77]. In most of those applications one is interested in codes with extremely low (ideally, constant) query complexity. For this reason, a lot of the work on locally decodable codes has concentrated on this regime. We follow the same tradition. In this book we study the trade-off between the length and the query complexity of LDCs, with emphasis on constant-query codes.

We conclude this section by presenting a family of k-query LDCs that encode messages of length n to codewords of length $\exp\left(n^{1/(k-1)}\right)$ for every n. This family (which generalizes the Hadamard code) is a classical example of locally decodable codes that can be traced back to [7, 10, 64, 73, 86]. Our presentation assumes that

---

[1] Throughout the book we use the standard notation $\exp(n) = 2^{O(n)}$.

the reader is familiar with some basic algebraic concepts such as finite fields and polynomials [31, 62].

1.1.2 A code based on polynomial interpolation

Fix $k \geq 2$ to be the desired query complexity. Pick a prime power $r \geq k+1$. Also, pick an integer $m \geq k-1$, and set $n = \binom{m}{k-1}$. We now show how to construct a k-query LDC encoding messages of length n over the finite field $\mathbb{F}_r$ to codewords of length r^m (over the same field). Note that for fixed k and growing m this yields codes of length $\exp\left(n^{1/(k-1)}\right)$.

We start with some notation. For a positive integer s, let $[s]$ denote the set $\{1, \ldots, s\}$. Let $\gamma : [n] \to \{0,1\}^m$ be a bijection between the set $[n]$ and the set of m-long $\{0,1\}$-vectors of Hamming weight $k-1$. (The Hamming weight of a vector is simply the number of its nonzero coordinates.) Finally, for $i \in [n]$ and $j \in [k-1]$ let $\gamma(i)_j$ denote the j-th nonzero coordinate of $\gamma(i)$.

Now we define the encoding procedure. Given a message $\mathbf{x} = (\mathbf{x}_1, \ldots, \mathbf{x}_n) \in \mathbb{F}_r^n$ consider a multivariate polynomial f in the ring $\mathbb{F}_r[z_1, \ldots, z_m]$,

$$f(z_1, \ldots, z_m) = \sum_{i=1}^n \mathbf{x}_i z_{\gamma(i)_1} \cdots z_{\gamma(i)_{k-1}}.$$

The key properties of the polynomial f are the following:

- f encodes the message: for every $i \in [n]$, we have $f(\gamma(i)) = \mathbf{x}_i$.
- f has low degree: $\deg f = k-1$.

We define the encoding of our message to be the evaluation of the polynomial f on the whole space $\mathbb{F}_r^m$. Clearly, such an encoding has length r^m.

It remains to show that the code defined above is indeed k-query locally decodable. Assume we are given an evaluation of the polynomial f over $\mathbb{F}_r^m$ that is adversarially corrupted in up to a fraction δ of the locations. We are also given some index $i \in [n]$ and want to recover $f(\mathbf{w})$, where $\mathbf{w} = \gamma(i)$, by probing the (corrupted) evaluation of f in at most k points.

Note that it does not make much sense to probe the value of f at the point $\mathbf{w}$ itself, since the value there may be corrupted. Instead, we obtain the value of $f(\mathbf{w})$ indirectly, relying on the rich structure of local dependences between the evaluations of a low-degree polynomial f at multiple points. Specifically, we randomly select an affine line $L \in \mathbb{F}_r^m$ containing the point $\mathbf{w}$ and issue queries asking for values of f at k distinct points of L. Next, we reconstruct the restriction of f to L. In particular, we recover the desired value $f(\mathbf{w})$. Below is a more formal description:

1. We pick a uniformly random vector $\mathbf{v} \in \mathbb{F}_r^m$.
2. We probe the evaluation of f at points $\mathbf{w} + \lambda \mathbf{v}$ for k distinct nonzero $\lambda \in \mathbb{F}_r$.

3. We interpolate a degree-$(k-1)$ univariate polynomial $f(\mathbf{w}+\lambda\mathbf{v}) \in \mathbb{F}_r[\lambda]$ using
   the values obtained above to get $f(\mathbf{w})$.

Observe that each individual point where we probe f in the decoding process is
uniformly random. Therefore, with probability at least $1-k\delta$, we never probe f at
a corrupted point, and decode correctly.

1.2 Private information retrieval schemes

The ubiquity of the Internet means a plethora of online public databases and an
indispensable resource for retrieving up-to-date information. But it also poses a sig-
nificant risk to user privacy, since a malicious database owner may monitor user
queries and infer what the user is after. Indeed, in cases where users' intentions
must be kept secret, users are often cautious about accessing public databases. For
example, investors querying a stock-market database for the current market value
of certain stocks might prefer not to reveal their interest in those stocks because
that could inadvertently influence their price. Alternatively, companies might want
to search for certain patents without revealing the identities of those patents. Private information retrieval schemes are cryptographic protocols that enable users to
retrieve records from public databases while keeping private the identity of the retrieved records.

For a reader who has not come across the notion of private information retrieval
schemes before, it may seem quite puzzling that one can retrieve database records
without revealing their identity to the server holding the database. Note, however,
that there is a trivial solution. Namely, whenever the user wants a single record, the
user can ask for a copy of the whole database. This solution involves a tremendous
communication overhead, and is clearly unacceptable in practice. It turns out [28]
that if the user wants to keep their privacy fully protected (in the information-
theoretic sense), then this trivial solution is essentially optimal.

Interestingly, the negative result above applies only to databases that are stored
on a single server (rather than being replicated across several servers). In a seminal
paper, Chor et al. [28] came up with PIR schemes that enable private retrieval of
records from replicated databases with a nontrivially small amount of communication. In such protocols, the user makes queries to each server holding the database.
The protocol ensures that each individual server (by observing only the query sent
to it) gets no information about the identity of the item the user is interested in.

Before going further, let us make the notion of a private information retrieval
scheme more concrete. We model a database as an n-bit string $\mathbf{x}$ that is replicated on
k noncommunicating servers. The user has an index i (which is an integer between 1
and n) and is interested in obtaining the value of the bit $\mathbf{x}_i$. To achieve this goal, the
user tosses some random coins, queries each of the servers, and gets replies, from
which the desired bit $\mathbf{x}_i$ can be computed. The query to each server is distributed
independently of i, and therefore each server gets no information about what the user
is after. The main parameters of interest in a PIR scheme are the number k of servers
involved, and the communication complexity, namely the number of bits exchanged

by a user accessing an n-bit database and the servers. The major goal of PIR-related research to design k-server PIR schemes with an optimal (i.e., the smallest possible) amount of communication for every k. In this book we work towards this goal, and obtain both positive and negative results regarding the communication complexity of private information retrieval schemes.

We conclude this section by presenting a concrete k-server PIR scheme due to David Woodruff and the author [95]. The scheme involves $O\left(n^{1/(2k-1)}\right)$ communication to access an n-bit database and is arguably the most intuitive among the currently known nontrivial PIR schemes. The ideas behind the scheme are very similar to those behind the locally decodable code of Section 1.1. Our presentation assumes that the reader is familiar with some basic algebraic concepts such as polynomials, finite fields, and derivatives [31, 62].

1.2.1 A PIR scheme based on polynomial interpolation

Fix $k \geq 1$ to be the desired number of servers. Pick a prime power $r \geq k + 1$. Also, pick an integer $m \geq 2k - 1$, and set $n = \binom{m}{2k-1}$. In what follows we obtain a k-server PIR scheme with $O(m)$ bits of communication to access a database of size n with entries from the finite field $\mathbb{F}_r$. Note that for fixed k and growing m this yields schemes with $O\left(n^{1/(2k-1)}\right)$ communication.

Following the technique from the example in Section 1.1, we pick $\gamma : [n] \rightarrow \{0,1\}^m$ to be a bijection between the set $[n]$ and the set of m-dimensional $\{0,1\}$-vectors of Hamming weight $2k - 1$. For $i \in [n]$ and $j \in [2k - 1]$, let $\gamma(i)_j$ denote the j-th nonzero coordinate of $\gamma(i)$. Given a database $\mathbf{x} = (\mathbf{x}_1, \ldots, \mathbf{x}_n) \in \mathbb{F}_r^n$ each server obtains the following polynomial f in the ring $\mathbb{F}_r[z_1, \ldots, z_m]$,

$$f(z_1, \ldots, z_m) = \sum_{i=1}^{n} \mathbf{x}_i z_{\gamma(i)_1} \cdots z_{\gamma(i)_{2k-1}}.$$

The key properties of the polynomial f are the following:

- f encodes the database: for every $i \in [n]$, we have $f(\gamma(i)) = \mathbf{x}_i$.
- f has low degree: $\deg f = 2k - 1$.

The basic idea behind our private information retrieval scheme is the idea of polynomial interpolation in a finite field setting. Suppose the user wants to retrieve the i-th coordinate of the database. Given i, the user computes the vector $\mathbf{w} = \gamma(i) \in \mathbb{F}_r^m$. Now the user's goal is to recover the value of the polynomial f (held by the servers) at the point $\mathbf{w}$.

Obviously, the user cannot explicitly request the value of f at $\mathbf{w}$ from any of the servers, since such a request would ruin the privacy of the protocol; that is, some server would get to know which database bit the user was after. Instead, the user obtains the value of $f(\mathbf{w})$ indirectly, relying on the rich structure of local dependences between the evaluations of a low-degree polynomial f at multiple points. Specifically, the user randomly selects an affine line $L \in \mathbb{F}_r^m$ containing the point $\mathbf{w}$ and discloses certain points on L to the servers. Each server computes and returns the value of f and the values of partial derivatives of f at the point that it has been given. Finally, the user reconstructs the restriction of f to L. In particular, the user obtains the desired value $f(\mathbf{w})$. Below is a more formal description.

We use the standard mathematical notation $(\partial f/\partial z_l)|_{\mathbf{y}}$ to denote the value of the partial derivative of f with respect to z_l at a point $\mathbf{y}$. Let $\lambda_1, \ldots, \lambda_k \in \mathbb{F}_r$ be distinct and nonzero. Let $\mathscr{U}$ denote the user and let $\mathscr{S}_1, \ldots, \mathscr{S}_k$ denote the servers. The protocol proceeds as follows:

$$
\begin{array}{ll}
\mathscr{U} & : \text{Picks } \mathbf{v} \in \mathbb{F}_r^m \text{ uniformly at random.} \\
\mathscr{U} \to \mathscr{S}_h & : \mathbf{w} + \lambda_h \mathbf{v} \\
\mathscr{U} \leftarrow \mathscr{S}_h & : f(\mathbf{w} + \lambda_h \mathbf{v}), \left.\dfrac{\partial f}{\partial z_1}\right|_{\mathbf{w}+\lambda_h\mathbf{v}}, \ldots, \left.\dfrac{\partial f}{\partial z_m}\right|_{\mathbf{w}+\lambda_h\mathbf{v}}
\end{array}
$$

Note that in the protocol above, the input to each server $\mathscr{S}_h, h \in [k]$, is a uniformly random point in $\mathbb{F}_r^m$. Therefore the protocol is private. It is also easy to verify that both the queries that the user sends to the servers and the servers' responses are of length $O(m) = O(n^{1/(2k-1)})$. (Every query is simply a point in $\mathbb{F}_r^m$. Every response is a list of m values of partial derivatives of f plus the value of f itself.) It remains to show how the user obtains $f(\mathbf{w})$ from the servers' responses.

Consider the line $L = \{\mathbf{w} + \lambda \mathbf{v} \mid \lambda \in \mathbb{F}_r\}$. Let $g(\lambda) = f(\mathbf{w} + \lambda \mathbf{v}) \in \mathbb{F}_r[\lambda]$ be the restriction of f to L. Clearly, $g(\lambda_h) = f(\mathbf{w} + \lambda_h \mathbf{v})$. Thus the user knows the values $\{g(\lambda_h)\}$ for all $h \in [k]$. However, the values $\{g(\lambda_h)\}$ do not suffice to reconstruct the polynomial g, since the degree of g may be up to $2k - 1$. The main observation underlying our protocol is that knowing the values of partial derivatives $(\partial f/\partial z_1)|_{\mathbf{w}+\lambda_h\mathbf{v}}, \ldots, (\partial f/\partial z_m)|_{\mathbf{w}+\lambda_h\mathbf{v}}$, the user can reconstruct the value of $g'(\lambda_h)$. The proof is a straightforward application of the chain rule:

$$
\left.\frac{\partial g}{\partial \lambda}\right|_{\lambda_h} = \left.\frac{\partial f(\mathbf{w} + \lambda \mathbf{v})}{\partial \lambda}\right|_{\lambda_h} = \sum_{l=1}^{m} \left.\frac{\partial f}{\partial z_l}\right|_{\mathbf{w}+\lambda_h\mathbf{v}} \mathbf{v}_l.
$$

Thus the user can reconstruct $\{g(\lambda_h)\}$ and $\{g'(\lambda_h)\}$ for all $h \in [k]$. Combining this observation with the standard algebraic fact that a univariate polynomial of degree $2k - 1$ is uniquely defined by its values and derivatives at k points [62], we conclude that the user can reconstruct g and obtain $\mathbf{x}_i = f(\mathbf{w}) = g(0)$.

1.3 The history of LDCs and PIR schemes

Both locally decodable codes and private information retrieval schemes can be seen as the combinatorial analogs of notions that had been studied in complexity theory in the late 1980s and early 1990s. In particular, the decoding procedures for locally decodable codes can be seen as a combinatorial version of self-correctors [22, 64], and private information retrieval schemes are analogous to instance-hiding schemes [4, 10, 11]. Private information retrieval schemes were introduced by Chor et al. [28] in 1995. Locally decodable codes were explicitly discussed in the PCP literature in early 1990s, most notably in [7, 73, 86]. However, the first formal definition of LDCs was given only in 2000, by Katz and Trevisan [56], who also recognized an intimate relationship between LDCs and PIR schemes. (Namely, that LDCs yield PIR schemes with related parameters and vice versa.) Since then, the study of LDCs and PIR schemes has grown into a fairly broad field, with many connections to other areas of theoretical computer science. There are two (somewhat outdated) surveys of the LDC/PIR literature available [43, 88]. See also [98].

One can informally classify the known families of LDCs and PIR schemes into three generations based on the technical ideas that underlie these constructions. The latest (third) generation is the main contribution of this book. In the following sections, we review every generation of codes and schemes and then proceed to lower bounds.

1.3.1 The first generation: interpolation

The first generation of locally decodable codes and private information retrieval schemes captures codes and schemes that are based on the idea of polynomial interpolation. Messages (databases) are encoded by complete evaluations of a low-degree multivariate polynomial over a finite field. Noise resilience (privacy) is achieved by reliance on the rich structure of short local dependences between such evaluations at multiple points. The codes and schemes presented in sections 1.1 and 1.2 belong to the first generation.

The ideas behind the first generation of codes and schemes [15, 56] can be traced back to the classical Reed–Muller codes [65, 89] that were introduced into coding theory in the 1960s. For constant query complexity $k \geq 2$, locally decodable codes of the first generation have a length $\exp\left(n^{1/(k-1)}\right)$.

There are a number of different PIR schemes of the first generation. The earliest such schemes are due to Chor et al. [28]. These schemes have communication complexity $O\left(n^{1/3}\right)$ in the case of two servers, and communication complexity $O(n^{1/k})$ in the general case of k servers. The recursive private information retrieval schemes of Ambainis [6] improve upon the schemes of [28] and attain communication complexity of $O\left(n^{1/(2k-1)}\right)$ in the case of k servers. (Note that the use of interpolation is implicit in both [28] and [6].) Other examples of PIR schemes of the first generation can be found in [15, 53, 95] and [17, Claims 3.1 and 3.2]. None of these schemes are recursive, and they have the same asymptotic parameters as the schemes of Ambainis [6].

1.3.2 The second generation: recursion

The second generation of locally decodable codes and private information retrieval schemes combines the earlier ideas of polynomial interpolation with a clever use of recursion. A PIR scheme of the second generation starts similarly to one of the first generation: the database is encoded by a complete evaluation of a certain low-degree multivariate polynomial over a finite field. However, the information retrieval procedure is rather different. Specifically, the user's queries are carefully crafted to ensure that there are substantial overlaps in the information that the user is sending to different servers. The user relies on such overlaps, and (in parallel) runs a few PIR subprotocols with (overlapping) groups of servers that share the same information. Finally, the user combines the information that he/she learns to obtain the desired value of the i-th bit.

The second generation of PIR schemes started with a breakthrough paper of Beimel et al. [17]. The constructions of [17] gave improved upper bounds for the communication complexity of k-server PIR schemes for all values of $k \geq 3$. In particular, Beimel et al. obtained three-server PIR schemes with $O(n^{1/5.25})$ communication; four-server PIR schemes with $O(n^{1/7.87})$ communication, and five-server PIR schemes with $O(n^{1/10.83})$ communication. For general k, they obtained k-server PIR schemes with $n^{O(\log\log k/k\log k)}$ asymptotic communication. Later, some of the results of [17] were given alternative proofs in the work of David Woodruff and the author [95], who also exploited an interplay between recursion and polynomial interpolation. The actual constructions of [17, 95] are quite involved; we do not include them in this book, but instead give a high-level overview of a specific three-server PIR scheme from [95].

Example scheme.

The scheme starts analogously to the PIR scheme described in Section 1.2. Given an n-bit database, each server $\{\mathscr{S}_h\}_{h \in [3]}$ represents it by a homogeneous degree-7 polynomial f in $m = O(n^{1/7})$ variables over some finite field $\mathbb{F}_r$. The user $\mathscr{U}$ holds a point $\mathbf{w} \in \mathbb{F}_r^m$ of Hamming weight 7 and wants to retrieve $f(\mathbf{w})$, while keeping the identity of $\mathbf{w}$ private. Rather than picking a random affine line containing the point $\mathbf{w}$, and sending some of its points to servers, the user picks a random two-dimensional affine plane π containing $\mathbf{w}$, and sends each server $\mathscr{S}_h$ a line L_h in π. We assume the lines $\{L_h\}_{h \in [3]}$ are in a general position. Note that now, for every pair of servers $\mathscr{S}_{h_1}, \mathscr{S}_{h_2}$, there is a point $L_{h_1} \cap L_{h_2} \in \pi$ that is known to both of them. The user exploits this fact, and for every pair of servers runs a separate two-server PIR protocol to obtain some algebraic information about the restriction of f to π. In addition, each server sends $\mathscr{U}$ the values and derivatives of the polynomial f at every point on its line. Finally, the user combines all received information to obtain the restriction of f to π.

The results of [17] gave rise to the second generation of locally decodable codes. Those codes are obtained from PIR schemes and have smaller lengths than the codes of the first generation for all values of query complexity $k \geq 4$. In particular, the authors of [17] obtained four-query LDCs of length $\exp(n^{3/10})$; five-query LDCs of length $\exp(n^{1/5})$, and six-query LDCs of length $\exp(n^{1/7})$. For general query complexity k, they achieved a length $\exp\left(n^{O(\log\log k/k\log k)}\right)$.

1.3.3 The third generation: point removal

The third generation of locally decodable codes and private information retrieval schemes is the main contribution of this book. Here, we introduce a new (point removal) approach to constructing locally decodable codes and obtain large improvements upon the earlier work. Our presentation is based on the key paper of the author [97] and the follow up work of Kiran Kedlaya and the author [57].

Our results.

- Given a Mersenne number $m = 2^t - 1$ that has a large prime factor $p > m^{0.75}$, we can design three-query LDCs of length $N = \exp\left(n^{1/t}\right)$, for every n. Based on the current state of knowledge about Mersenne primes (i.e., primes of the form $2^t - 1$), this translates to a length of less than $\exp\left(n^{10^{-7}}\right)$, compared with $\exp\left(n^{1/2}\right)$ in the previous constructions. Our results for three-query LDCs yield improvements of similar magnitude for larger values of query complexity k, via the generic reduction given in [17].
- It has often been conjectured that there are infinitely many Mersenne primes. Under this conjecture, our constructions yield three-query locally decodable codes of length $N = \exp\left(n^{O(1/\log\log n)}\right)$ for infinitely many n. Under a stronger (yet well accepted) conjecture [2, 74, 90] regarding the density of Mersenne primes, our constructions yield three-query locally decodable codes of length $N = \exp\left(n^{O\left(1/\log^{1-\varepsilon}\log n\right)}\right)$ for all n, for every $\varepsilon > 0$.
- Our improvements in the parameters of locally decodable codes yield analogous improvements for private information retrieval schemes. We have given three-server PIR schemes with communication complexity of $O\left(n^{10^{-7}}\right)$ to access an n-bit database, compared with the previous best scheme, with complexity $O(n^{1/5.25})$. Assuming again that there are infinitely many Mersenne primes, we get three-server PIR schemes of communication complexity $n^{O(1/\log\log n)}$ for infinitely many n. Finally, assuming the above conjecture regarding the density of Mersenne primes, we get three-server PIR schemes of communication complexity $n^{O(1/\log^{1-\varepsilon}\log n)}$ for all n, for every $\varepsilon > 0$.

The results above were not expected by the community. After a decade of effort, many researchers in the area were pessimistic and believed that locally decodable codes with constant query complexity and subexponential length, and private information retrieval schemes with a constant number of servers and subpolynomial communication do not exist. In particular, such conjectures were published explicitly in [43, section 9] and [47, conjecture 4.4].

Our technique.

All previously known constructions of locally decodable codes and private information retrieval schemes are (explicitly or implicitly) centered around the idea of representing a message by an evaluation of a certain low-degree polynomial over a finite field. Our constructions take a completely different approach.

We start by reducing the problem of constructing locally decodable codes to the problem of designing certain families of sets with restricted intersections. We next give a (basic) construction of such families that relies on linear algebra over finite fields. Our basic construction does not yield improved parameters for LDCs, but has a simple geometric intuition underlying it: our universe is a high-dimensional linear space (over a finite field), and our sets are lines and (unions of) affine hyperplanes. Our key insight, which gives the that gives the name to the method, is that one can perform surgery on the basic construction and greatly improve its parameters. Specifically, one can carefully *remove most of the points from lines* while preserving the right intersection properties.

The problem one needs to solve in order to successfully accomplish point removal is the following: one needs to design a set $S \subseteq \mathbb{F}_p^*$ for prime p that simultaneously satisfies two properties. (1) There exist two large sequences of vectors $u_1, \ldots, u_n, v_1, \ldots, v_n$ in some low-dimensional space $\mathbb{F}_p^m$, such that the dot products $(u_i, v_i) = 0$ for all i, and the dot products $(u_j, v_i) \in S$ for all $i \neq j$. We refer to this property as the "combinatorial niceness" of S. (2) For a small integer k, there exists a k-sparse polynomial $\phi(x) \in \mathbb{F}_2[x]$ such that the common GCD of all polynomials of the form $\phi(x^\beta)$, $\beta \in S$, and the polynomial $x^p - 1$ is nontrivial. We refer to this property as the "algebraic niceness" of S.

Our construction of locally decodable codes thus has three steps. First, we show that a set S exhibiting both combinatorial and algebraic niceness leads to good locally decodable codes. In particular, the length n of the sequences $u_1, \ldots, u_n$ and $v_1, \ldots, v_n$ corresponds to the number of message bits that we can encode, while the length of the codewords that we build is $N = p^m$. So the longer the sequence and the smaller the dimension the better. The query complexity of our codes is given by the parameter k from the definition of the algebraic niceness of S. This step of our construction is quite general and applies to vectors $u_1, \ldots, v_n$ and subsets S over any field. It leads us to the task of identifying good sets that are both combinatorially and algebraically nice, and these tasks narrow our choice of fields. As our second step we focus on combinatorial niceness. In general, big sets tend to be "nicer" (allow longer sequences) than small ones. We show that every multiplicative subgroup of a prime field is as combinatorially as nice as its cardinality would allow. This still leaves us with a variety of fields and subsets to work with. Finally, as the last step, we develop an insight into the algebraic niceness of sets. We focus on the very narrow case of primes p that are large prime factors of Mersenne numbers, and the subgroup generated by the element 2 in $\mathbb{F}_p^*$. We manage to show that this subgroup is nice enough to get three-query locally decodable codes, leading to our final result.

An alternative view of our constructions can be found in the follow-up work of Raghavendra [75].

Mersenne primes.

As one can see above, our results for locally decodable codes and private information retrieval schemes rely heavily on known results regarding Mersenne numbers with large prime factors (and, in particular, on known results regarding Mersenne primes). To the best of the author's knowledge, our results are the first applications of Mersenne primes outside of number theory. We now briefly review the history of Mersenne primes starting from ancient times. We also summarize the current knowledge regarding these numbers. Our exposition mostly follows [3].

Many ancient cultures were concerned with the relationship of a number to the sum of its divisors. Positive numbers that are equal to the sum of all of their positive divisors (excluding the number itself) were called *perfect*. Perfect numbers were often given mystical interpretations. The first four perfect numbers are $6 = 1+2+3$, $28 = 1+2+4+7+14$, 496, and 8128. By looking at the prime factorization of these four numbers one can observe that each of them has the form $2^{t-1}(2^t - 1)$, where t is an integer and $2^t - 1$ is prime. This is not a coincidence. About 2300 years ago Euclid proved that every number of such form is perfect. (Much later, Euler proved a partial converse, namely that an *even* number is perfect if and only if it has the form $2^{t-1}(2^t - 1)$, where $2^t - 1$ is prime.)

The connection to perfect numbers outlined above motivated mathematicians to look more closely at prime numbers of the form $2^t - 1$. One of the mathematicians who were interested in such primes was the French monk Marin Mersenne (1588–1648). In the preface to his book *"Cogitata Physica-Mathematica"* (1644) Mersenne stated that the numbers $2^t - 1$ were prime for

$$t = 2, 3, 5, 7, 13, 17, 19, 31, 67, 127 \text{ and } 257$$

and were composite for all other positive integers $t < 257$. Mersenne's conjecture was incorrect (he missed $61, 89$, and 107 and included 67 and 257, which do not yield primes). Despite that, nowadays integers of the form $2^t - 1$ are called Mersenne numbers, and primes of such a form are called Mersenne primes.

Apart from the connection to perfect numbers, the other reasons why Mersenne primes are so appealing are their succinctness and (since the late 1870s) the existence of the very efficient deterministic Lucas–Lehmer [78] primality test for integers of the form $2^t - 1$. The study of Mersenne primes that started hundreds of years ago is still ongoing. One part of this activity is a search for large Mersenne primes. Nowadays, this search involves using powerful modern computers. One of the notable contributors to the search is George Woltman. In 1996 he had the idea of using the Internet to coordinate this search and developed the Great Internet Mersenne Prime Search (GIMPS) project, which allows amateurs to join the search by donating some of the computational power of their personal computers. The GIMPS project has been quite successful: it has found a total of ten Mersenne primes, each of which was the largest known prime at the time of discovery. The largest known prime, as of June 2007, is $2^{32\,582\,657} - 1$. This Mersenne prime was discovered on September 4, 2006 by Steven Boone and Curtis Cooper [1].

Although the study of Mersenne primes has a very long history, so far mathematicians do not have answers to even the most basic questions regarding these numbers. In particular, it is not known whether the number of Mersenne primes is infinite. There is a feeling in the math community that it may take a long time before this question is resolved [81]. A widely accepted conjecture states that (once found) the answer will be affirmative (i.e., there are infinitely many Mersenne primes). In fact, much stronger conjectures regarding the density of Mersenne primes have been made by Lenstra, Pomerance, and Wagstaff [2, 74, 90]. When we present our results for locally decodable codes and private information retrieval schemes, we shall give both unconditional results (based on the largest known Mersenne prime) and conditional results (under the assumption that the number of Mersenne primes is infinite).

1.3.4 Lower bounds

The existing lower bounds on the length of locally decodable codes fit the following high-level strategy. Firstly, one converts a given locally decodable code into a *smooth* code, i.e., a code where each query of the decoder is distributed (nearly) uniformly over the set of codeword coordinates. Secondly, one employs either classical combinatorial tools such as isoperimetric inequalities and random restrictions [32, 48, 56, 70] or (quantum) information theory inequalities [58, 91, 93] to obtain a bound on the length of the smooth code.

The first lower bounds on the length of locally decodable codes were obtained by Katz and Trevisan [56]. Further work on lower bounds includes [32, 48, 58, 70, 91, 93]. The length of optimal two-query LDCs was settled by Kerenidis and de Wolf in [58] and is exponential in the message length. However, for values of query complexity $k \geq 3$ we are still very far from closing the gap between lower and upper bounds. Specifically, the best lower bounds to date are of the form $\tilde{\Omega}\left(n^{1+1/(\lceil k/2 \rceil - 1)}\right)$ due to Woodruff [93], while the best upper bounds are $\exp\left(n^{O_k(1/\log\log n)}\right)$ [97] even under number-theoretic conjectures.

Progress in lower bounds on the communication complexity of private information retrieval schemes has also been quite scarce. In what follows, we list the known results for the two-server case. The first nontrivial lower bound of $4 \log n$ was due to

Mann [66]. Later, this was improved to $4.4 \log n$ by Kerenidis and de Wolf [58]. The current record of $5 \log n$ is due to Wehner and de Wolf [91]. This leaves us with a tremendous gap to the best upper bound of $O\left(n^{1/3}\right)$ [28].

It is quite interesting to note that the upper bound above has never been improved upon since the initial paper of Chor et al. [28] in 1995. Although to date a number of different two-server PIR schemes are known [15, 28, 95], all of them have the same communication complexity.

Apart from the work on general lower bounds for PIR protocols, there has been some effort to establish (stronger) lower bounds for various restricted models of PIR [14, 48, 54, 76]. In particular, Itoh [54] obtained polynomial lower bounds on the communication complexity of one round PIR, under the assumption that each server returns a multilinear or affine function of its input. Goldreich et al. [48] introduced the notion of *linear* PIR protocols, i.e., protocols where the servers are restricted to returning linear combinations of the database bits to the user, and also the notion of *probe complexity*, i.e., the maximum number of bits that the user needs to read from servers' answers in order to compute x_i. Goldreich et al. obtained polynomial lower bounds for the communication complexity of two-server linear PIR schemes whose probe complexity is constant. Later, their results were extended by Wehner and de Wolf [91], who showed that the restriction of linearity can in fact be dropped.

Another restricted form of two-server PIR was considered by Alexander Razborov and the author [76], who showed that every bilinear group-based PIR scheme requires $\Omega\left(n^{1/3}\right)$ communication. A bilinear PIR scheme is a one-round, two-server PIR scheme, where the user computes the dot product of the servers' responses to obtain the desired value of the i-th bit. A group-based PIR scheme is a PIR scheme that involves servers representing the database by a function on a certain finite group G, and allows the user to retrieve the value of this function for any group element using a natural secret-sharing scheme based on G. The model of bilinear group-based PIR generalizes all PIR protocols known to date [76, Appendix]. In Chapter 4 of this book we present the results of [76] in full detail.

1.4 Applications of LDCs and PIR schemes

Earlier in this chapter, we talked about the application of locally decodable codes to data transmission and storage. We also discussed the natural application of private information retrieval schemes. In this section, we review some of the most notable other applications of LDCs and PIR schemes.

1.4.1 Secure multiparty computation

A fundamental result of Ben-Or, Goldwasser, and Wigderson [21] and Chaum, Crepeau, and Damgard [26] dating from 1988 asserts that information-theoretic secure multiparty computation is feasible. Specifically, in [21, 26] it was shown that $k \geq 3$ players who are allowed to exchange messages over secure channels can jointly compute any function of their local inputs while hiding those inputs from each other; i.e., one can always arrange a protocol to ensure that after the joint computation has been performed, any specific player gets no information about the inputs of other players (apart from the information contained in the value of the function).

In all known protocols for secure multiparty computation, the communication complexity of the protocol grows linearly with the circuit size of the function being computed. This results in $\exp(n)$ communication for securely computing most of the functions of n-bit inputs. A natural question that was explicitly asked in several papers in the late 1980s and early 1990s [11, 12] was whether *all* functions can be securely computed with only a polynomial (or at least a subexponential) amount of communication in the input length. It was observed by Ishai and Kushilevtiz [52] that this question is closely related to the complexity of private information retrieval schemes.

Our constructions of PIR schemes with a subpolynomial amount of communication yield the first quantitative progress on the question outlined above (via the reduction given in [52]). Specifically, our results imply that a group of 18 or more players can securely compute any function of their n-bit inputs with a total communication of $\exp\left(n/\log^{1-\varepsilon} n\right)$, for all n, and for every $\varepsilon > 0$, assuming the Lenstra–Pomerance–Wagstaff conjecture [2, 74, 90] regarding the density of Mersenne primes.

1.4.2 Other models of private information retrieval

A large number of extensions of the basic PIR model have been studied. These include extensions to t-private protocols, in which the user is protected against collusions of up to t servers [9, 15, 28]; extensions which protect the servers holding the database (in addition to the user), termed symmetric PIR [46, 69]; and other extensions [18, 19, 25, 33, 45, 71]. In almost all extensions, the best-known solutions are obtained by adding some extra layers on top of a basic private information retrieval scheme. Therefore improving the parameters of (basic) PIR schemes yields improvements for many other problems. For instance, see [9] for a construction of improved t-private PIR schemes, based on PIR schemes from this book.

Computational PIR.

The private information retrieval schemes discussed in the previous sections are often called "information-theoretic" because they provide an absolute guarantee that each server participating in the protocol execution gets no information about what the users are after. PIR has also been studied in a computational setting [16, 24, 34, 44, 59, 60, 61, 63, 72, 83]. Computational PIR schemes are similar to their information-theoretic counterparts but provide a weaker guarantee. Specifically, they ensure only that a server cannot get any information about a user's intent unless it solves a computationally hard problem (such as factoring a large random integer). Providing privacy or security guarantees based on computational hardness assumptions is common in modern cryptography. In contrast to information-theoretic PIR schemes, computational PIR protocols with a low communication overhead exist (under standard assumptions), even when a database is stored on a single server. However, for typical real-life parameters, the known computational protocols are less efficient than the known information-theoretic ones [17].

Computational and information-theoretic PIR schemes rely on different sets of techniques. While our main focus in this book is on information-theoretic schemes, (and thus we reserve the term "PIR" for information-theoretic protocols), we give below a high-level overview of an early computational PIR scheme due to Kushilevitz and Ostrovsky [60].

This scheme relies on a standard hardness assumption, the quadratic residuosity assumption. Let m be a positive integer. A number a is called a quadratic residue, or QR, modulo m, if there exists an integer x such that $x^2 = a \bmod m$. Otherwise, a is called a quadratic nonresidue, or QNR, modulo m. The QR assumption states that it is computationally hard to distinguish numbers that are QRs modulo m from those that are not, unless one knows the factorization of m.

The protocol.

The server stores the n-bit database $\mathbf{x}$ in a square matrix of size $s \times s$ for $s = \sqrt{n}$:

$$\begin{bmatrix} \mathbf{x}_{11} & \cdots & \mathbf{x}_{1j} & \cdots & \mathbf{x}_{1s} \\ \vdots & & \vdots & & \vdots \\ \mathbf{x}_{i1} & \cdots & \mathbf{x}_{ij} & \cdots & \mathbf{x}_{is} \\ \vdots & & \vdots & & \vdots \\ \mathbf{x}_{s1} & \cdots & \mathbf{x}_{sj} & \cdots & \mathbf{x}_{ss} \end{bmatrix} \begin{bmatrix} a_1 \\ \vdots \\ b_i \\ \vdots \\ a_s \end{bmatrix}$$

Suppose the database user is interested in obtaining the value $\mathbf{x}_{ij}$ for some i, j between 1 and s. The user selects a large integer m together with its factorization at random and generates $s-1$ random QRs $a_1, \ldots, a_{i-1}, a_{i+1}, \ldots, a_s$ modulo m, as well as a single random QNR b_i. The user then sends the string $a_1, \ldots, a_{i-1}, b_i, a_{i+1}, \ldots, a_s$ and the integer m to the server. The QR assumption implies that the server cannot distinguish b_i from integers $\{a_l\}$ and thus observes only a string of s random-looking integers $u_1, \ldots, u_s$ modulo m (one for each row of the database). The server responds with s integers $\pi_1, \ldots, \pi_s$ (one for each column of the database). Here each π_h is equal to a product of integers u_l for all l such that $\mathbf{x}_{lh} = 1$; formally, $\pi_h = \prod_{l \mid x_{lh}=1} u_l \bmod m$.

Verifying that the value of π_j is going to be a QR modulo m if $\mathbf{x}_{ij} = 0$ and is going to be a QNR modulo m if $\mathbf{x}_{ij} = 1$ is not hard, since a product of two QRs is a QR and the product of a QR with a QNR is a QNR. The user need only check whether π_j is a QR, which is easy, since the user knows the factorization of m.

The total amount of communication in this PIR scheme is roughly $O(\sqrt{n})$. Better computational PIR protocols are available; see [44, 63] for the most efficient computational PIR schemes known to date.

1.4.3 Average-case complexity

One of the earliest applications of locally decodable codes was to worst-case-to-average-case reductions in computational complexity theory. This application requires LDCs with polynomial length and polylogarithmic query complexity. Such codes have been known to exist since 1990s [7, 8, 87] (in fact they predate the formal introduction of LDCs in [56]) and can be obtained by certain modifications [88, Section 3.4] of the classical Reed–Muller codes [65, 89]. Our review of an example application of LDCs to worst-case-to-average-case reductions mostly follows [88, Section 3.5].

Let L be an EXP-complete problem, and for an input length t let us consider the restriction of L to inputs of length t. We can see L, restricted to these inputs, as a binary string of length 2^t. Let us encode this string using a polynomial-length locally decodable code C that has polylogarithmic query complexity and can tolerate some constant fraction of errors. We get a string of length $2^{O(t)} = 2^{t'}$, and let us think of this string as defining a new problem L' on inputs of length t'. If L is in EXP, then so is L'. The properties of the code C imply that a polynomial-time algorithm for L' that is good on average (i.e., solves L' correctly on, say, some fraction $1 - \varepsilon$ of the inputs in polynomial time) yields a probabilistic algorithm for L that works on all inputs, and EXP $\subseteq$ BPP. This argument shows that if every problem in EXP can be solved well on average, then EXP $\subseteq$ BPP. A similar statement can be proved for PSPACE using a variant of this argument.

1.5 Organization of the book

The main contribution of this book is a novel *point removal* approach to constructing locally decodable codes that yields large improvements upon earlier work. In Chapter 2 we give a detailed treatment of the approach, and present our main results for LDCs. Chapter 3 deals with the potential and limitations of the point removal approach. We argue that further progress in the unconditional bounds via this method (under a fairly broad definition of the method) would imply progress on an old number theory question regarding the size of the largest prime factors of Mersenne numbers. Although Chapters 2 and 3 are based on [57, 97], they contain some previously unpublished results. Specifically, in this book we consider locally decodable codes over general (not necessarily binary) alphabets.

The last Chapter 4, contains our results for private information retrieval schemes. We start by presenting large improvements in upper bounds for PIR schemes involving three or more servers (which follow from improved upper bounds for LDCs). We then turn to the natural question regarding whether two-server PIR is truly intrinsically different. We argue that this may well be the case. We introduce a novel combinatorial approach to PIR and establish the optimality of the currently best-known two-server schemes using a restricted although fairly broad model. The lower-bounds part of Chapter 4 is based on [76].

1.6 Addendum

Following the initial publication of the thesis in 2007, there has been a large amount of follow-up work extending the results obtained here in various directions. We summarize the most important developments below.

- Building on Raghavendra's view of locally decodable codes of the third generation [75], Efremenko [38] generalized the code construction to work over composites. Efremenko [38] relied on a powerful combinatorial construction of Grolmusz [49, 50] and, for every positive integer $t \geq 2$, obtained a family of 2^t-query LDCs of length $\exp\left(\exp\left((\log n)^{1/t}(\log\log n)^{1-1/t}\right)\right)$. He also obtained the first family of three-query LDCs that unconditionally have subexponential length. Later, Itoh and Suzuki [55] showed that in certain cases the query complexity of the codes described in [38] can be reduced.
- In [36], Dvir et al. studied the parameters of locally decodable codes of the third generation in the regime of super-constant query complexity. They proved that the LDCs of the third generation are superior to the LDCs of earlier generations for query complexities smaller than $\log n/(\log\log n)^{O(1)}$, and that the LDCs of the third generation are inferior those of the first generation for query complexities larger than $(\log n)^{\Omega(\sqrt{\log n})}$. Later, some of the results in [36] were independently rediscovered and extended by Ben-Aroya et al. [20], who also considered local list decoding.
- Woodruff [94] and Gal and Mills [42] obtained a number of results relating the query complexity and codeword length of locally decodable codes to the probability of a decoding error.

Recently, locally decodable codes have found new applications in the areas of lower bounds for arithmetic circuits [35], data structures [27, 30], and derandomization [37].

Chapter 2
Locally decodable codes via the point removal method

This chapter contains a detailed exposition of the point removal method for constructing locally decodable codes. The method can be broken into two parts. The first part is a reduction that shows how the existence of subsets of finite fields that simultaneously exhibit "nice" properties of two different kinds yields families of locally decodable codes with good parameters. The second part is a construction of "nice" subsets of finite fields.

Sections 2.1 and 2.2 of this chapter are preliminary. In Section 2.3, we give a detailed treatment of the first part of our method for the narrow case of binary codes. We treat binary codes separately to have a simpler setup where we can (in an intuitive yet formal manner) demonstrate the combinatorial and geometric ideas that lie behind our method. While we believe that Section 2.3 may be the most important part of the book (since it explains the intuition behind our approach), it can be skipped by the reader who is interested only in a succinct formal treatment of the constructions. After a detailed treatment of binary codes in Section 2.3, we give a succinct treatment of general codes in Section 2.4. As our main conclusion, we identify the two "nice" properties of subsets of finite fields that (simultaneously) yield good codes. We call those properties combinatorial and algebraic niceness.

The next two sections cover the second part of our method. In Section 2.5, we construct combinatorially nice subsets of prime fields, and in Section 2.6 we construct algebraically nice subsets of prime fields. Finally, in Section 2.7, we put the results of the previous sections together and summarize our improvements in upper bounds for locally decodable codes.

2.1 Notation

We use the following standard mathematical notation:

- $[s] = \{1, \ldots, s\}$.
- $\mathbb{Z}_n$ denotes integers modulo n.

S. Yekhanin, *Locally Decodable Codes and Private Information Retrieval Schemes*,
Information Security and Cryptography, DOI 10.1007/978-3-642-14358-8_2,
© Springer-Verlag Berlin Heidelberg 2010

- $\mathbb{F}_q$ is a finite field of q elements.
- $\mathbb{F}_q^*$ is the multiplicative group of $\mathbb{F}_q$.
- $d_H(\mathbf{x}, \mathbf{y})$ denotes the Hamming distance between vectors $\mathbf{x}$ and $\mathbf{y}$.
- $(\mathbf{u}, \mathbf{v})$ stands for the dot product of vectors $\mathbf{u}$ and $\mathbf{v}$.
- For a linear space $L \subseteq \mathbb{F}_r^m$, $L^\perp$ denotes the *dual* space. That is,

$$L^\perp = \{\mathbf{u} \in \mathbb{F}_r^m \mid \forall \mathbf{v} \in L, (\mathbf{u}, \mathbf{v}) = 0\}.$$

2.2 Locally decodable codes

In this section we formally define locally decodable codes.

Definition 1. An r-ary code $C : [r]^n \to [r]^N$ is said to be (k, δ, ε)-locally decodable if there exists a randomized decoding algorithm $\mathscr{A}$ such that:

1. For all $\mathbf{x} \in [r]^n$, $i \in [n]$ and $\mathbf{y} \in [r]^N$ such that $d_H(C(\mathbf{x}), \mathbf{y}) \leq \delta N$,

$$\Pr[\mathscr{A}^{\mathbf{y}}(i) = \mathbf{x}_i] \geq 1 - \varepsilon,$$

   where the probability is taken over the random coin tosses of the algorithm $\mathscr{A}$.
2. $\mathscr{A}$ makes at most k queries to $\mathbf{y}$.

In the special case when r is a prime power and the elements of the alphabet $[r]$ are in one-to-one correspondence with the elements of the finite field $\mathbb{F}_r$, it makes sense to talk about *linear* codes. A locally decodable code C is called linear if C is a linear transformation over $\mathbb{F}_r$. In this book we consider only codes over prime alphabets, and all our codes are linear.

2.3 Binary LDCs via point removal

In this section, we give a detailed treatment of the first part of our method for the narrow case of binary codes. Our goal here is to explain the intuition behind the point removal approach; therefore, we gradually build up our main construction, trying to provide motivation for every choice that we make. Our final result is a claim that subsets of prime fields that exhibit certain properties (combinatorial and algebraic niceness) yield families of LDCs with very good parameters.

In Section 2.3.1, we introduce certain combinatorial objects that we call regular intersecting families of sets. These objects later serve as our tool to construct binary LDCs. In Section 2.3.2, we present a linear algebraic construction of a regular intersecting family that yields locally decodable codes with good (although not the best known) parameters. The notions of combinatorial and algebraic niceness of sets are used implicitly in this section. Our main construction in Section 2.3.3 builds upon the construction of Section 2.3.2 via the *point removal* procedure. We formally introduce combinatorial and algebraic niceness and show how the interplay between these two notions yields locally decodable codes.

2.3.1 Regular intersecting families of sets

The locally decodable codes that we construct are linear. Our decoding algorithms proceed by tossing random coins, reading a certain k-tuple of coordinates of the (corrupted) codeword, and outputting the XOR of the values at these coordinates.

Observe that every linear LDC encoding n-bit messages to N-bit codewords admits a combinatorial description. Let N, R, and n be arbitrary positive integers. For $i \in [n]$, let $\mathbf{e}^i$ denote a binary n-dimensional (unit) vector, whose unique nonzero coordinate is i. In order to define a k-query linear locally decodable code, it is sufficient to specify the following for every $i \in [n]$:

- A set $T_i \subseteq [N]$ of coordinates of $C(\mathbf{e}^i)$ that are set to 1. Such sets completely specify the encoding, since for any message $\mathbf{x}$, $C(\mathbf{x}) = \sum_{i:\mathbf{x}_i=1} C(\mathbf{e}^i)$.
- A family $\{Q_{ir}\}, r \in [R]$, of subsets of $[N]$ of size k that specify collections of codeword coordinates that can be read by a decoding algorithm in order to reconstruct the i-th message bit.

Clearly, not every collection of sets $\{T_i\}$ and $\{Q_{ir}\}$ yields a locally decodable code. Certain combinatorial constraints must be satisfied. We formally define these constraints below.

Definition 2. We say that the subsets $\{T_i\}$ and $\{Q_{ir}\}$ form a (k, n, N, R, s)-regular intersecting family if the following conditions are satisfied:

1. k is odd.
2. For all $i \in [n]$, $|T_i| = s$.
3. For all $i \in [n]$ and $r \in [R]$, $|Q_{ir}| = k$.
4. For all $i \in [n]$ and $r \in [R]$, $Q_{ir} \subseteq T_i$.
5. For all $i \in [n]$ and $w \in T_i$, $|\{r \in [R] \mid w \in Q_{ir}\}| = (Rk)/s$, (i.e., T_i is uniformly covered by the sets Q_{ir}).
6. For all $i, j \in [n]$ and $r \in [R]$ such that $i \neq j$, $|Q_{ir} \cap T_j| \equiv 0 \mod (2)$.

We now formally show how regular intersecting families yield binary locally decodable codes.

Proposition 1. *A (k, n, N, R, s)-regular intersecting family yields a binary linear code encoding n bits to N bits that is $(k, \delta, \delta Nk/s)$-locally decodable for all δ.*

Proof. For a set $S \subseteq [N]$, let $I(S) \in \{0, 1\}^N$ denote its *incidence vector*. Formally, for $w \in [N]$, we set $I(S)_w = 1$ if $w \in S$, and $I(S)_w = 0$ otherwise. We define a linear code C via its generator matrix $G \in \{0, 1\}^{n \times N}$. For $i \in [n]$, we set the i-th row of G to be the incidence vector of the set T_i. Below is the description of the decoding algorithm $\mathscr{A}$. Given oracle access to $\mathbf{y}$ and input $i \in [n]$, the algorithm $\mathscr{A}$ does the following.

1. It picks $r \in [R]$ uniformly at random.
2. It outputs the dot product $(\mathbf{y}, I(Q_{ir}))$ over $\mathbb{F}_2$.

Note that since $|Q_{ir}| = k$, $\mathscr{A}$ needs only k queries to $\mathbf{y}$ to compute the dot product. It is easy to verify that the decoding is correct if $\mathscr{A}$ picks $r \in [R]$ such that all bits of $\mathbf{x}G$ in locations $h \in Q_{ir}$ are not corrupted:

$$(\mathbf{x}G, I(Q_{ir})) = \sum_{j=1}^{n} \mathbf{x}_j (I(T_j), I(Q_{ir})) = \mathbf{x}_i (I(T_i), I(Q_{ir})) = \mathbf{x}_i. \qquad (2.1)$$

The second equality in (2.1) follows from part 6 of Definition 2 and the last equality follows from parts 1, 3 and 4 of Definition 2.

Now assume that up to δN bits of the encoding $\mathbf{x}G$ have been corrupted. Part 5 of Definition 2 implies that there are at most $(\delta NRk)/s$ sets Q_{ir} that contain at least one corrupted location. Thus, with probability at least $1 - (\delta Nk)/s$, the algorithm $\mathscr{A}$ outputs the correct value.   □

To the best of our knowledge, regular intersecting families of sets have not been studied previously. The closest combinatorial objects that have some literature are Ruzsa–Szemerédi (hyper)graphs [40, 79, 80].

2.3.2 Basic construction

In this section we present our basic construction of regular intersecting families, which yields binary k-query locally decodable codes of length $\exp\left(n^{1/(k-1)}\right)$ for prime values of $k \geq 3$. Note that for $k > 3$, the parameters that we get are inferior to the parameters of LDCs of the second generation (see Section 1.3.2).

There is a strong geometric intuition underlying our construction. We choose our universe $[N]$ to be a high-dimensional linear space over a prime field $\mathbb{F}_p$. We choose the sets $\{T_i\}$ to be unions of cosets of certain hyperplanes, and the sets $\{Q_{ir}\}$ to be affine lines. We argue the intersection properties based on elementary linear algebra. Let p be an odd prime, and let $m \geq p - 1$ be an integer.

Lemma 1. *Let* $n = \binom{m}{p-1}$. *There exist two families of vectors* $\{\mathbf{u}_1, \dots, \mathbf{u}_n\}$ *and* $\{\mathbf{v}_1, \dots, \mathbf{v}_n\}$ *in* $\mathbb{F}_p^m$ *such that*

- *For all* $i \in [n]$, $(\mathbf{u}_i, \mathbf{v}_i) = 0$.
- *For all* $i, j \in [n]$ *such that* $i \neq j$, $(\mathbf{u}_j, \mathbf{v}_i) \neq 0$.

Proof. Let $\mathbf{e} \in \mathbb{F}_p^m$ be the vector that contains 1's in all the coordinates. We set the vectors $\{\mathbf{u}_i\}$ to be the incidence vectors of all possible $\binom{m}{p-1}$ subsets of $[m]$ of cardinality $(p-1)$. For every $i \in [n]$, we set $\mathbf{v}_i = \mathbf{e} - \mathbf{u}_i$. It is straightforward to verify that this family satisfies the condition of the lemma.   □

Now we are ready to present our regular intersecting family. We set $N = p^m$ and $n = \binom{m}{p-1}$. We assume some bijection between the set $[N]$ and the space $\mathbb{F}_p^m$. For $i \in [n]$, we set

$$T_i = \left\{ \mathbf{w} \in \mathbb{F}_p^m \mid (\mathbf{u}_i, \mathbf{w}) \in \mathbb{F}_p^* \right\}.$$

We set

$$R = s = (p-1) \cdot p^{m-1}.$$

For each $i \in [n]$, we assume some bijection between points of T_i and elements of $[R]$. For $i \in [n]$ and $r \in [R]$, let $\mathbf{w}_{ir}$ be the r-th point of T_i. We set

$$Q_{ir} = \left\{ \mathbf{w}_{ir} + \lambda \mathbf{v}_i \mid \lambda \in \mathbb{F}_p \right\}.^1$$

Lemma 2. *For $i \in [n]$ and $r \in [R]$, the sets $\{T_i\}$ and $\{Q_{ir}\}$ defined above form a (p, n, N, R, s)-regular intersecting family.*

Proof. We simply need to verify that all six conditions listed in Definition 2 are satisfied.

1. Condition 1 is trivial.
2. Condition 2 is trivial.
3. Condition 3 is trivial.
4. Fix $i \in [n]$ and $r \in [R]$. Given that $(\mathbf{u}_i, \mathbf{w}_{ir}) \in \mathbb{F}_p^*$ let us show that $Q_{ir} \subseteq T_i$. By Lemma 1, $(\mathbf{u}_i, \mathbf{v}_i) = 0$. Thus, for every $\lambda \in \mathbb{F}_p$,

$$(\mathbf{u}_i, \mathbf{w}_{ir} + \lambda \mathbf{v}_i) = (\mathbf{u}_i, \mathbf{w}_{ir}).$$

   Condition 4 follows.
5. Fix $i \in [n]$ and $\mathbf{w} \in T_i$. Note that

$$\left| \{ r \in [R] \mid \mathbf{w} \in Q_{ir} \} \right| = \left| \{ \mathbf{w}_{ir} \in T_i \mid \exists \lambda \in \mathbb{F}_p, \mathbf{w} = \mathbf{w}_{ir} + \lambda \mathbf{v}_i \} \right|$$
$$= \left| \{ \mathbf{w}_{ir} \in T_i \mid \exists \lambda \in \mathbb{F}_p, \mathbf{w}_{ir} = \mathbf{w} - \lambda \mathbf{v}_i \} \right| = p.$$

   It remains to note that $Rp/s = p$. Condition 5 follows.
6. Fix $i, j \in [n]$, and $r \in [R]$ such that $i \neq j$. Note that

$$\left| Q_{ir} \cap T_j \right| = \left| \{ \lambda \in \mathbb{F}_p \mid (\mathbf{u}_j, \mathbf{w}_{ir} + \lambda \mathbf{v}_i) \in \mathbb{F}_p^* \} \right|$$
$$= \left| \{ \lambda \in \mathbb{F}_p \mid ((\mathbf{u}_j, \mathbf{w}_{ir}) + \lambda(\mathbf{u}_j, \mathbf{v}_i)) \in \mathbb{F}_p^* \} \right| = p - 1.$$

   The last equality follows from the fact that $(\mathbf{u}_j, \mathbf{v}_i) \neq 0$, and therefore the univariate linear function $(\mathbf{u}_j, \mathbf{w}_{ir}) + \lambda(\mathbf{u}_j, \mathbf{v}_i)$ takes every value in $\mathbb{F}_p$ exactly once. It remains to note that $p - 1$ is even. Condition 6 follows.

This completes the proof. □

Combining Lemma 2 and Proposition 1 we get the following corollary.

---

[1] Note that the sets Q_{ir} are not all distinct.

Corollary 1. *Let p be an odd prime and let $m \geq p - 1$ be an integer. There exists a binary linear code encoding $\binom{m}{p-1}$ bits to p^m bits that is $\left(p, \delta, \delta p^2/(p-1)\right)$-locally decodable for all δ.*

It is now easy to convert the above result into a *dense family* (i.e., one that has a code for every message length n, as opposed to infinitely many n's) of p-query LDCs of length $\exp\left(n^{1/(p-1)}\right)$.

Theorem 1. *Let p be a fixed odd prime. For every positive integer n there exists a code of length $\exp\left(n^{1/(p-1)}\right)$ that is $\left(p, \delta, \delta p^2/(p-1)\right)$-locally decodable for all δ.*

Proof. Given n, choose m to be the smallest integer such that $n \leq \binom{m}{p-1}$. Set $n' = \binom{m}{p-1}$. It is easy to verify that if n is sufficiently large, we have $n' \leq 2n$. Given a message $\mathbf{x}$ of length n, we pad it with zeros to a length n' and use the code in Corollary 1 that encodes $\mathbf{x}$ with a codeword of length $p^m = \exp\left(n^{1/(p-1)}\right)$.   □

2.3.3 The main construction: point removal

In the previous section, we presented our basic linear algebraic construction of regular intersecting families of sets. We chose the sets $\{T_i\}$ to be unions of cosets of certain hyperplanes. We chose the sets $\{Q_{ir}\}$ to be affine lines.

The high-level idea behind our main construction is to reduce the number of codeword locations queried by *removing some points from lines*; i.e., by choosing the sets $\{Q_{ir}\}$ to be *proper subsets of lines* rather than whole lines while preserving the right intersection properties.

Before we proceed to our main construction, we introduce two central technical concepts of our method, namely *combinatorial* and *algebraic niceness* of sets. We now give some narrow definitions that are needed to construct binary codes via the point removal method in linear spaces over prime fields. Later, in Section 2.4 we shall give more general definitions. Let p be an odd prime.

Definition 3. A set $S \subseteq \mathbb{F}_p^*$ is called (m,n)-*combinatorially nice* if there exist two families of vectors $\{\mathbf{u}_1, \ldots, \mathbf{u}_n\}$ and $\{\mathbf{v}_1, \ldots, \mathbf{v}_n\}$ in $\mathbb{F}_p^m$ such that:

- For all $i \in [n]$, $(\mathbf{u}_i, \mathbf{v}_i) = 0$.
- For all $i, j \in [n]$ such that $i \neq j$, $(\mathbf{u}_j, \mathbf{v}_i) \in S$.

Remark 1. Note that in Lemma 1 we established that the set $S = \mathbb{F}_p^*$ is $\left(m, \binom{m}{p-1}\right)$-combinatorially nice for every integer $m \geq p - 1$.

Definition 4. A set $S \subseteq \mathbb{F}_p$ is called k-*algebraically nice* if k is odd and there exist two sets $S_0, S_1 \subseteq \mathbb{F}_p$ such that:

- S_0 is not empty.

- $|S_1| = k$.
- For all $\alpha \in \mathbb{F}_p$ and $\beta \in S$, $|S_0 \cap (\alpha + \beta S_1)| \equiv 0 \bmod (2)$.

Remark 2. It is easy to verify that the set $S = \mathbb{F}_p^*$ is p-algebraically nice. We simply pick $S_1 = \mathbb{F}_p$ and $S_0 = \mathbb{F}_p^*$.

The next lemma shows how an interplay between combinatorial and algebraic niceness yields regular intersecting families. It is the core of our construction.

Lemma 3. *Assume that $S \subseteq \mathbb{F}_p^*$ is simultaneously (m,n)-combinatorially nice and k-algebraically nice. Let S_0 be the set in the definition of the algebraic niceness of S. The set S yields a $\left(k, n, p^m, |S_0|p^{m-1}, |S_0|p^{m-1}\right)$-regular intersecting family.*

Proof. For $i \in [n]$, let $\mathbf{u}_i, \mathbf{v}_i$ be the vectors in the definition of combinatorial niceness. Set $N = p^m$ and
$$R = s = |S_0|p^{m-1}.$$
Assume a bijection between $[N]$ and $\mathbb{F}_p^m$. For all $i \in [n]$, set
$$T_i = \left\{ \mathbf{w} \in \mathbb{F}_p^m \mid (\mathbf{u}_i, \mathbf{w}) \in S_0 \right\}.$$

For each $i \in [n]$, assume some bijection between $[R]$ and T_i. Let $\mathbf{w}_{ir}$ denote the r-th point of T_i. Set
$$Q_{ir} = \{\mathbf{w}_{ir} + \lambda \mathbf{v}_i \mid \lambda \in S_1\}.$$

It remains to verify that all six conditions listed in Definition 2 are satisfied.

1. Condition 1 is trivial.
2. Condition 2 is trivial.
3. Condition 3 is trivial.
4. Fix $i \in [n]$ and $r \in [R]$. Given that $(\mathbf{u}_i, \mathbf{w}_{ir}) \in S_0$, let us show that $Q_{ir} \subseteq T_i$. Definition 3 implies that $(\mathbf{u}_i, \mathbf{v}_i) = 0$. Thus, for every $\lambda \in S_1$,

$$(\mathbf{u}_i, \mathbf{w}_{ir} + \lambda \mathbf{v}_i) = (\mathbf{u}_i, \mathbf{w}_{ir}).$$

Condition 4 follows.
5. Fix $i \in [n]$ and $\mathbf{w} \in T_i$. Note that

$$|\{r \in [R] \mid \mathbf{w} \in Q_{ir}\}| = |\{\mathbf{w}_{ir} \in T_i \mid \exists \lambda \in S_1, \mathbf{w} = \mathbf{w}_{ir} + \lambda \mathbf{v}_i\}|$$
$$= |\{\mathbf{w}_{ir} \in T_i \mid \exists \lambda \in S_1, \mathbf{w}_{ir} = \mathbf{w} - \lambda \mathbf{v}_i\}| = |S_1| = k.$$

It remains to note that $Rk/s = k$. Condition 5 follows.
6. Fix $i, j \in [n]$ and $r \in [R]$ such that $i \neq j$. Note that

$$|Q_{ir} \cap T_j| = |\{\lambda \in S_1 \mid (\mathbf{u}_j, \mathbf{w}_{ir} + \lambda \mathbf{v}_i) \in S_0\}|$$
$$= |\{\lambda \in S_1 \mid ((\mathbf{u}_j, \mathbf{w}_{ir}) + \lambda(\mathbf{u}_j, \mathbf{v}_i)) \in S_0\}|$$
$$= |S_0 \cap ((\mathbf{u}_j, \mathbf{w}_{ir}) + (\mathbf{u}_j, \mathbf{v}_i)S_1)| \equiv 0 \bmod (2).$$

The last equality follows from the fact that $(\mathbf{u}_j, \mathbf{v}_i) \in S$, and Definition 4. Condition 6 follows.

This completes the proof.   □

Observe that one can derive a regular intersecting family with the parameters of Lemma 2 using Lemma 3 in combination with Remarks 1 and 2.

The next proposition, which follows immediately by combining Proposition 1 with Lemma 3 is the heart of the first part of our construction of LDCs (for the case of binary codes).

Proposition 2. *Let p be an odd prime. Assume that $S \subseteq \mathbb{F}_p^*$ is simultaneously (m,n)-combinatorially nice and k-algebraically nice. Let S_0 be the set in the definition of the algebraic niceness of S. The set S yields a binary linear code encoding n bits to p^m bits that is $(k, \delta, \delta pk/|S_0|)$-locally decodable for all δ.*

Later, we will see that for every Mersenne prime $p = 2^t - 1$, the multiplicative subgroup generated by the element 2 in $\mathbb{F}_p^*$ is three-algebraically nice (Lemma 14) and sufficiently combinatorially nice (Lemma 6) to yield three-query LDCs of length $\exp\left(n^{1/t}\right)$ via the proposition above.

2.4 General LDCs via point removal

In this section, we present a general treatment of the first part of our construction of locally decodable codes. We extend the results of the previous section in two ways: (1) we consider codes over alphabets $\mathbb{F}_r$, for arbitrary primes r, rather than only binary codes; (2) we consider nice subsets of arbitrary finite fields $\mathbb{F}_q$, rather than only prime fields. We start by defining the combinatorial and algebraic niceness of subsets in the general setup, and then proceed to a succinct formal proof of the main propositions.

Definition 5. *Let q be a prime power. A set $S \subseteq \mathbb{F}_q^*$ is called (m,n)-combinatorially nice if there exist two families of vectors $\{\mathbf{u}_1, \ldots, \mathbf{u}_n\}$ and $\{\mathbf{v}_1, \ldots, \mathbf{v}_n\}$ in $\mathbb{F}_q^m$ such that:*

- *For all $i \in [n]$, $(\mathbf{u}_i, \mathbf{v}_i) = 0$.*
- *For all $i, j \in [n]$ such that $i \neq j$, $(\mathbf{u}_j, \mathbf{v}_i) \in S$.*

In many cases, it will be more convenient for us to use the following definition of combinatorial niceness that involves a single parameter t.

Definition 6. *Let q be a prime power. A set $S \subseteq \mathbb{F}_q^*$ is called t-combinatorially nice if for some $c > 0$ and every positive integer m, S is $(m, \lfloor cm^t \rfloor)$-combinatorially nice.*

Given a map f from a finite set to a field let $\mathrm{supp}(f)$ denote its *support* i.e., the number of elements of the set that are not mapped to zero. Now we proceed to the general definition of algebraic niceness.

Definition 7. Let q be a prime power and r be a prime. A set $S \subseteq \mathbb{F}_q^*$ is called k-algebraically nice over $\mathbb{F}_r$ if there exist two maps, $S_0 : \mathbb{F}_q \to \mathbb{F}_r$ and $S_1 : \mathbb{F}_q \to \mathbb{F}_r$ such that:

- $\mathrm{supp}(S_0) \neq 0$.
- $\mathrm{supp}(S_1) \leq k$.
- $\sum\limits_{\lambda \in \mathbb{F}_q} S_1(\lambda) \neq 0$.
- For all $\alpha \in \mathbb{F}_q$ and $\beta \in S$, $\sum\limits_{\lambda \in \mathbb{F}_q} S_0(\alpha + \beta\lambda)S_1(\lambda) = 0$.

We now proceed to our core lemma, which shows how sets exhibiting both combinatorial and algebraic niceness yield locally decodable codes.

Lemma 4. *Let q be a prime power and let r be a prime. Assume that $S \subseteq \mathbb{F}_q^*$ is simultaneously (m,n)-combinatorially nice, and k-algebraically nice over $\mathbb{F}_r$. Let S_0 be the map in the definition of the algebraic niceness of S. The set S yields an $\mathbb{F}_r$-linear code encoding messages of length n to codewords of length q^m that is $(k, \delta, \delta qk/\mathrm{supp}(S_0))$-locally decodable for all δ.*

Proof. Our proof has three steps. We specify encoding and local decoding procedures for our codes and then argue a lower bound for the probability of correct decoding. We use notation from Definitions 5 and 7.

Encoding. Our code will be linear. Therefore it suffices to specify the encoding of *unit vectors* $\mathbf{e}_1, \dots, \mathbf{e}_n$, where $\mathbf{e}_j$ has length n and a unique nonzero coordinate j. We define the encoding of $\mathbf{e}_j$ to be a vector of length q^m, whose coordinates are labeled by elements of $\mathbb{F}_q^m$. For all $\mathbf{w} \in \mathbb{F}_q^m$, we set

$$\mathrm{Enc}(\mathbf{e}_j)_\mathbf{w} = S_0((\mathbf{u}_j, \mathbf{w})). \tag{2.2}$$

Local decoding. Suppose that the decoding algorithm $\mathscr{A}$ needs to recover the i-th coordinate of the message, $i \in [n]$. To simplify the notation, we put

$$c = \frac{1}{\left(S_0((\mathbf{u}_i, \mathbf{w})) \sum\limits_{\lambda \in \mathbb{F}_q} S_1(\lambda) \right)}.$$

Given a (possibly corrupted) codeword $\mathbf{y}$, $\mathscr{A}$ picks $\mathbf{w} \in \mathbb{F}_q^m$ such that $S_0((\mathbf{u}_i, \mathbf{w})) \neq 0$ uniformly at random, reads $\mathrm{supp}(S_1) \leq k$ coordinates of $\mathbf{y}$, and outputs the sum

$$c \sum_{\lambda \in \mathbb{F}_q : S_1(\lambda) \neq 0} S_1(\lambda) \mathbf{y}_{\mathbf{w} + \lambda \mathbf{v}_i}. \tag{2.3}$$

Probability of correct decoding. First we argue that the decoding is always correct if $\mathscr{A}$ picks $\mathbf{w} \in \mathbb{F}_q^m$ such that all coordinates of $\mathbf{y}$ with labels in the set $\{\mathbf{w} + \lambda \mathbf{v}_i\}_{\lambda : S_1(\lambda) \neq 0}$ are not corrupted. We need to show that for all $i \in [n]$, $\mathbf{x} \in \mathbb{F}_r^n$, and $\mathbf{w} \in \mathbb{F}_q^m$, such that $S_0((\mathbf{u}_i, \mathbf{w})) \neq 0$,

$$c \sum_{\lambda \in \mathbb{F}_q : S_1(\lambda) \neq 0} S_1(\lambda) \left(\sum_{j=1}^{n} \mathbf{x}_j \operatorname{Enc}(\mathbf{e}_j) \right)_{\mathbf{w} + \lambda \mathbf{v}_i} = \mathbf{x}_i. \qquad (2.4)$$

Note that

$$
\begin{aligned}
& c \sum_{\lambda \in \mathbb{F}_q} S_1(\lambda) \left(\sum_{j=1}^{n} \mathbf{x}_j \operatorname{Enc}(\mathbf{e}_j) \right)_{\mathbf{w} + \lambda \mathbf{v}_i} \\
&= c \sum_{j=1}^{n} \mathbf{x}_j \left(\sum_{\lambda \in \mathbb{F}_q} S_1(\lambda) \operatorname{Enc}(\mathbf{e}_j)_{\mathbf{w} + \lambda \mathbf{v}_i} \right) \qquad (2.5) \\
&= c \sum_{j=1}^{n} \mathbf{x}_j \left(\sum_{\lambda \in \mathbb{F}_q} S_1(\lambda) S_0((\mathbf{u}_j, \mathbf{w} + \lambda \mathbf{v}_i)) \right).
\end{aligned}
$$

Now note that

$$\sum_{\lambda \in \mathbb{F}_q} S_1(\lambda) S_0((\mathbf{u}_j, \mathbf{w} + \lambda \mathbf{v}_i)) = \sum_{\lambda \in \mathbb{F}_q} S_1(\lambda) S_0((\mathbf{u}_j, \mathbf{w}) + \lambda (\mathbf{u}_j, \mathbf{v}_i))$$

$$= \begin{cases} 1/c, & \text{if } i = j, \\ 0, & \text{otherwise.} \end{cases}$$

For $i = j$, the last identity above follows from $(\mathbf{u}_i, \mathbf{v}_i) = 0$ and the definition of the constant c. For $i \neq j$, the identity follows from $(\mathbf{u}_j, \mathbf{v}_i) \in S$ and the algebraic niceness of S. Combining (2.5) with the identity above, we get (2.4).

Now assume that up to a fraction δ of the coordinates of $\mathbf{y}$ are corrupted. Let T_i denote the set of coordinates whose labels belong to

$$\{ \mathbf{w} \in \mathbb{F}_q^m \mid S_0((\mathbf{u}_i, \mathbf{w})) \neq 0 \}.$$

It is not hard to see that $|T_i| = q^{m-1} \operatorname{supp}(S_0)$. Thus at most a fraction $\delta q / \operatorname{supp}(S_0)$ of the coordinates in T_i are corrupted. Let

$$Q_i = \left\{ \{ \mathbf{w} + \lambda \mathbf{v}_i \}_{\lambda \in \mathbb{F}_q : S_1(\lambda) \neq 0} \mid \mathbf{w} : S_0((\mathbf{u}_i, \mathbf{w})) \neq 0 \right\}$$

be the family of $\operatorname{supp}(S_1)$-tuples of coordinates that may be queried by $\mathscr{A}$. $(\mathbf{u}_i, \mathbf{v}_i) = 0$ implies that the elements of Q_i uniformly cover the set T_i. Combining the last two observations, we conclude that with probability at least $1 - \delta q k / \operatorname{supp}(S_0)$, $\mathscr{A}$ picks an uncorrupted $\operatorname{supp}(S_1) \leq k$-tuple and outputs the correct value of $\mathbf{x}_i$. $\qquad \square$

The parameters of the locally decodable code that one gets by applying Lemma 4 to a (nice) set S depend on the support of S_0, where S_0 is the map in the definition of the algebraic niceness of S. The next lemma shows that one can always ensure that the support of S_0 is large, and thus obtain a good dependence of the decoding error on the fraction of corrupted locations.

Lemma 5. *Let q be a prime power and let r be a prime. Let $S \subseteq \mathbb{F}_q^*$ be a k-algebraically nice set over $\mathbb{F}_r$. Let S_0, S_1 be the maps in the definition of the algebraic niceness of S. One can always redefine the map S_0 to satisfy $\mathrm{supp}(S_0) \geq \lceil q(1 - 1/r) \rceil$.*

Proof. The algebraic niceness of S implies that for all $\alpha \in \mathbb{F}_q$ and $\beta \in S$,

$$\sum_{\lambda \in \mathbb{F}_q} S_0(\alpha + \beta\lambda) S_1(\lambda) = 0.$$

Equivalently, for all $\alpha \in \mathbb{F}_q$ and $\beta \in S$,

$$\sum_{\lambda \in \mathbb{F}_q} S_0(\lambda) S_1((\lambda - \alpha)\beta^{-1}) = 0. \tag{2.6}$$

Our goal is to redefine the map S_0 to satisfy both (2.6) and $\mathrm{supp}(S_0) \geq \lceil q(1 - 1/r) \rceil$.

Consider a linear space $M = \mathbb{F}_r^q$ where the coordinates of vectors are labeled by elements of $\mathbb{F}_q$. Note that there is a natural one-to-one correspondence between vectors in M and maps from $\mathbb{F}_q$ to $\mathbb{F}_r$. Specifically, a map $f : \mathbb{F}_q \to \mathbb{F}_r$ corresponds to a vector $\mathbf{v} \in M$ such that $\mathbf{v}_\lambda = f(\lambda)$ for all $\lambda \in \mathbb{F}_q$.

Let $L \subseteq M$ be a linear subspace spanned by the vectors corresponding to all maps $f(\lambda) = S_1((\lambda - \alpha)\beta^{-1})$, where $\alpha \in \mathbb{F}_q$ and $\beta \in S$. Observe that L is invariant under the actions of a 1-transitive permutation group (that is permuting the coordinates in accordance with addition in $\mathbb{F}_q$). This implies that the dual space $L^\perp$ is also invariant under the actions of the same group. Note that $L^\perp$ has positive dimension since it contains the vector corresponding to the map S_0. The last two observations imply that $L^\perp$ has *full support*, i.e., for every $i \in [q]$ there exists a vector $\mathbf{v} \in L^\perp$ such that $\mathbf{v}_i \neq 0$. It is easy to verify that any linear subspace of $\mathbb{F}_r^q$ that has full support contains a vector of Hamming weight at least $\lceil q(1 - 1/r) \rceil$. Let $\mathbf{v} \in L^\perp$ be such a vector. By redefining the map S_0 to be the map from $\mathbb{F}_q$ to $\mathbb{F}_r$ corresponding to the vector $\mathbf{v}$, we conclude the proof. $\qquad\square$

The following propositions are the heart of the first part of our construction of LDCs. Combining Lemmas 4 and 5, we get the following proposition.

Proposition 3. *Let q be a prime power and let r be a prime. Assume that $S \subseteq \mathbb{F}_q^*$ is simultaneously (m, n)-combinatorially nice, and k-algebraically nice over $\mathbb{F}_r$. The set S yields an $\mathbb{F}_r$-linear code encoding messages of length n to codewords of length q^m that is $(k, \delta, \delta k r/(r-1))$-locally decodable for all δ.*

Using proposition 3 in combination with the single-parameter definition of combinatorial niceness, we get the following proposition.

Proposition 4. *Let q be a prime power and let r be a prime. Assume that $S \subseteq \mathbb{F}_q^*$ is simultaneously t-combinatorially nice, and k-algebraically nice over $\mathbb{F}_r$; then, for every $n > 0$ there exists an $\mathbb{F}_r$-linear code encoding messages of length n to codewords of length $\exp\left(n^{1/t}\right)$ that is $(k, \delta, \delta k r/(r-1))$-locally decodable for all δ.*

Proof. Let $c > 0$ be the constant in the (single-parameter) definition of the combinatorial niceness of S. Given a message of length n, we pad it with zeros to get a message of length n', where $n' \geq n$ is the smallest integer of the form $\lfloor cm^t \rfloor$, and then use the code in proposition 3. It is not hard to verify that the padding results in at most a constant (multiplicative) blowup in the message length, and thus the length of our code is $\exp\left(n^{1/t}\right)$. $\square$

Propositions 3 and 4 identify two properties of subsets of finite fields that together yield good locally decodable codes. These properties are combinatorial and algebraic niceness. Our next goal is to construct nice subsets. In the next sections, we show that if the primes p and r are such that p is a large factor of $r^t - 1$, then the multiplicative subgroup generated by the number r in $\mathbb{F}_p^*$ is sufficiently (algebraically and combinatorially) nice to yield constant-query LDCs of length $\exp\left(n^{1/t}\right)$ over $\mathbb{F}_r$ for all message lengths n.

2.5 Combinatorially nice subsets of $\mathbb{F}_p^*$

In this section we study combinatorial niceness and show that multiplicative subgroups of prime fields are combinatorially nice.

For $\mathbf{w} \in \mathbb{F}_p^m$ and a positive integer l, let $\mathbf{w}^{\otimes l} \in \mathbb{F}_p^{m^l}$ denote the l-th tensor power of $\mathbf{w}$. The coordinates of $\mathbf{w}^{\otimes l}$ are labeled by all possible sequences in $[m]^l$, and

$$\mathbf{w}^{\otimes l}_{i_1,\ldots,i_l} = \prod_{j=1}^{l} \mathbf{w}_{i_j}.$$

Our next goal is to establish the following lemma.

Lemma 6. *Let p be a prime and let $m \geq p - 1$ be an integer. Suppose that S is a subgroup of $\mathbb{F}_p^*$; then S is $\left(\binom{m-1+(p-1)/|S|}{(p-1)/|S|}, \binom{m}{p-1}\right)$-combinatorially nice.*

Proof. Let $n = \binom{m}{p-1}$. For $i \in [n]$, let the vectors $\mathbf{u}_i''$ and $\mathbf{v}_i''$ in $\mathbb{F}_p^m$ be the same as the vectors $\mathbf{u}_i, \mathbf{v}_i$ in the proof of Lemma 1, i.e., the vectors $\mathbf{u}_i''$ are incidence vectors of all possible subsets of $[m]$ of cardinality $(p-1)$, and the vectors $\mathbf{v}_i''$ are their complements. Recall that:

- For all $i \in [n]$, $(\mathbf{u}_i'', \mathbf{v}_i'') = 0$.
- For all $i, j \in [n]$ such that $i \neq j$, $(\mathbf{u}_j'', \mathbf{v}_i'') \neq 0$.

Let l be a positive integer and let $\mathbf{u}, \mathbf{v}$ be vectors in $\mathbb{F}_p^m$. Observe that

$$\left(\mathbf{u}^{\otimes l}, \mathbf{v}^{\otimes l}\right) = \sum_{(i_1,\dots,i_l)\in[m]^l} \left(\prod_{j=1}^{l} \mathbf{u}_{i_j} \prod_{j=1}^{l} \mathbf{v}_{i_j}\right)$$

$$\tag{2.7}$$

$$= \sum_{(i_1,\dots,i_l)\in[m]^l} \left(\prod_{j=1}^{l} \mathbf{u}_{i_j}\mathbf{v}_{i_j}\right) = \left(\sum_{i_1\in[m]} \mathbf{u}_{i_1}\mathbf{v}_{i_1}\right)\cdots\left(\sum_{i_l\in[m]} \mathbf{u}_{i_l}\mathbf{v}_{i_l}\right) = (\mathbf{u},\mathbf{v})^l.$$

Let $l = (p-1)/|S|$. For $i \in [n]$ set $\mathbf{u}_i' = \mathbf{u}_i''^{\otimes l}$ and $\mathbf{v}_i' = \mathbf{v}_i''^{\otimes l}$. Equation (2.7) and the fact that $\mathbb{F}_p^*$ is a cyclic group yield the following:

- For all $i \in [n]$, $(\mathbf{u}_i', \mathbf{v}_i') = 0$.
- For all $i, j \in [n]$ such that $i \neq j$, $(\mathbf{u}_j', \mathbf{v}_i') \in S$.

Note that the vectors $\mathbf{u}_i'$ and $\mathbf{v}_i'$ have $m^{(p-1)/|S|}$ coordinates. Therefore, at this point, we have already shown that the set S is $\left(m^{(p-1)/|S|}, \binom{m}{p-1}\right)$-combinatorially nice.

Let $\mathbf{w}$ be an arbitrary vector in $\mathbb{F}_p^m$. Note that the value of $\mathbf{w}_{i_1,\dots,i_l}^{\otimes l}$ depends on the *multiset* $\{i_1,\dots,i_l\}$ rather than the sequence $i_1,\dots,i_l$. Thus many coordinates of $\mathbf{w}^{\otimes l}$ contain identical (and therefore redundant) values. We are going to reduce the number of coordinates in the vectors $\{\mathbf{u}_i'\}$ and $\{\mathbf{v}_i'\}$ using this observation. Let $F(m,l)$ denote the family of all multi-subsets of $[m]$ of cardinality l. Note that

$$|F(m,l)| = \binom{m-1+l}{l}.$$

For a multiset $\sigma \in F(m,l)$, let $c(\sigma)$ denote the number of sequences in $[m]^l$ that represent σ. Now we are ready to define the vectors $\{\mathbf{u}_i\}$ and $\{\mathbf{v}_i\}$ in $\mathbb{F}_p^{|F(m,l)|}$. The coordinates of the vectors $\{\mathbf{u}_i\}$ and $\{\mathbf{v}_i\}$ are labeled by multisets $\sigma \in F(m,l)$. For all $i \in [n]$ and $\sigma \in F(m,l)$, we set

$$(\mathbf{u}_i)_\sigma = c(\sigma)(\mathbf{u}_i')_\sigma \text{ and } (\mathbf{v}_i)_\sigma = (\mathbf{v}_i')_\sigma.$$

It is easy to verify that for all $i, j \in [n]$, $(\mathbf{u}_j, \mathbf{v}_i) = \left(\mathbf{u}_j', \mathbf{v}_i'\right)$. Combining this observation with the properties of the vectors $\mathbf{u}_i'$ and $\mathbf{v}_i'$ that were established earlier, we conclude that the set S is $\left(\binom{m-1+(p-1)/|S|}{(p-1)/|S|}, \binom{m}{p-1}\right)$-combinatorially nice. $\qquad\square$

We now give a simple corollary to Lemma 6 that uses a single-parameter definition of combinatorial niceness.

Lemma 7. *Let p be a prime. Suppose that S is a multiplicative subgroup of $\mathbb{F}_p^*$; then S is $|S|$-combinatorially nice.*

Proof. Let $t = |S|$. We need to specify a constant $c > 0$ such that for every positive integer m, there exist two collections of size $n = \lfloor cm^t \rfloor$-sized of m-dimensional vectors over $\mathbb{F}_p$ satisfying:

- For all $i \in [n]$, $(\mathbf{u}_i, \mathbf{v}_i) = 0$.

- For all $i, j \in [n]$ such that $i \neq j$, $(\mathbf{u}_j, \mathbf{v}_i) \in S$.

First, assume that m has the form $m = \binom{m'-1+(p-1)/t}{(p-1)/t}$, for some integer $m' \geq p -$ 1. In this case Lemma 6 gives us a collection of $n = \binom{m'}{p-1}$ vectors with the right properties. Observe that $n \geq cm^t$ for a constant c that depends only on p and t. Now assume that m does not have the right form, and let m_1 be the largest integer smaller than m that does have the right form. In order to get vectors of dimension m, we use vectors of dimension m_1, obtained from Lemma 6 padded with zeros. It is not hard to verify that such a construction still gives us families of vectors of size $n \geq cm^t$ for a suitably chosen constant c.   □

2.6 Algebraically nice subsets of $\mathbb{F}_p^*$

In the previous section, we studied the concept of combinatorial niceness and established that multiplicative subgroups of prime fields are combinatorially nice. In this section we study the concept of algebraic niceness, and show that (under certain constraints on p and r) the multiplicative subgroup generated by r in $\mathbb{F}_p^*$ is algebraically nice over $\mathbb{F}_r$.

We start by introducing some notation. Let p and r be distinct primes.

- The order of r modulo p, which is commonly denoted by $\mathrm{ord}_p(r)$, is the smallest integer t such that $p \mid r^t - 1$.
- $\langle r \rangle \subseteq \mathbb{F}_p^*$ denotes the multiplicative subgroup of $\mathbb{F}_p^*$ generated by the element r. Clearly, $|\langle r \rangle| = \mathrm{ord}_p(r)$.
- $\overline{\mathbb{F}}$ denotes the algebraic closure of the field $\mathbb{F}$.
- $C_r^p \subseteq \overline{\mathbb{F}}_r^*$ denotes the multiplicative subgroup of p-th roots of unity in $\overline{\mathbb{F}}_r$.

Definition 8. Let p and r be distinct primes. We say that there is a *nontrivial k-dependence* between the elements of C_r^p if there exist $\zeta_1, \ldots, \zeta_k \in C_r^p$ and $\sigma_1, \ldots, \sigma_k \in \mathbb{F}_r$ such that

$$\sigma_1 \zeta_1 + \ldots + \sigma_k \zeta_k = 0 \quad \text{and} \quad \sigma_1 + \ldots + \sigma_k \neq 0. \tag{2.8}$$

Lemma 8. *Let p and r be distinct primes. Suppose there exists a nontrivial k-dependence between the elements of C_r^p; then $\langle r \rangle \subseteq \mathbb{F}_p^*$ is k-algebraically nice over the field $\mathbb{F}_r$.*

Proof. In what follows, we define a map $S_1 : \mathbb{F}_p \to \mathbb{F}_r$ and prove the existence of a map $S_0 : \mathbb{F}_p \to \mathbb{F}_r$ such that, together, S_0 and S_1 yield k-algebraic niceness of $\langle r \rangle$ over $\mathbb{F}_r$. The identity (2.8) implies that for some $k' \leq k$ there exist k' *distinct* p-th roots of unity $\zeta_1, \ldots, \zeta_{k'} \in C_r^p$ such that for some $\sigma_1, \ldots, \sigma_{k'} \in \mathbb{F}_r$,

$$\sigma_1 \zeta_1 + \ldots + \sigma_{k'} \zeta_{k'} = 0 \quad \text{and} \quad \sigma_1 + \ldots + \sigma_{k'} \neq 0. \tag{2.9}$$

Let $t = \mathrm{ord}_p(r)$. Observe that $C_r^p \subseteq \mathbb{F}_{r^t}$. Let g be a multiplicative generator of C_r^p. The identity (2.9) yields

$$\sigma_1 g^{\gamma_1} + \ldots + \sigma_{k'} g^{\gamma_{k'}} = 0,$$

for some distinct values $\{\gamma_i\}_{i \in [k']}$ in $\mathbb{Z}_p$. We define

$$S_1(\lambda) = \begin{cases} \sigma_i, & \text{if } \lambda = \gamma_i, \text{ for some } i \in [k'], \\ 0, & \text{otherwise.} \end{cases}$$

The identity (2.9) yields $\mathrm{supp}(S_1) \leq k$ and

$$\sum_{\lambda \in \mathbb{F}_p} S_1(\lambda) \neq 0.$$

Now our goal is to prove the existence of a (nonzero) map $S_0 : \mathbb{F}_p \to \mathbb{F}_r$ such that for all $\alpha \in \mathbb{F}_p$ and $\beta \in S$,

$$\sum_{\lambda \in \mathbb{F}_p} S_0(\alpha + \beta\lambda) S_1(\lambda) = 0.$$

Equivalently, we need (a nonzero) map S_0 such that for all $\alpha \in \mathbb{F}_p$ and $\beta \in S$,

$$\sum_{\lambda \in \mathbb{F}_p} S_0(\lambda) S_1((\lambda - \alpha)\beta^{-1}) = 0. \tag{2.10}$$

Consider a natural one-to-one correspondence between maps $S' : \mathbb{F}_p \to \mathbb{F}_r$ and polynomials $\phi_{S'}(x)$ in the ring $\mathbb{F}_r[x]/(x^p - 1)$,

$$\phi_{S'}(x) = \sum_{\lambda \in \mathbb{Z}_p} S'(\lambda) x^\lambda.$$

Clearly, for every map $S' : \mathbb{F}_p \to \mathbb{F}_r$ and every fixed $\alpha, \beta \in \mathbb{F}_p$ such that $\beta \neq 0$,

$$\phi_{S'((\lambda - \alpha)\beta^{-1})}(x) = \sum_{\lambda \in \mathbb{F}_p} S'((\lambda - \alpha)\beta^{-1}) x^\lambda$$

$$= \sum_{\lambda \in \mathbb{F}_p} S'(\lambda) x^{\alpha + \beta\lambda} = x^\alpha \phi_{S'}(x^\beta).$$

Let α be a variable ranging over $\mathbb{F}_p$, and let β be a variable ranging over $\langle r \rangle$. We are going to argue the existence of a map $S_0 : \mathbb{F}_p \to \mathbb{F}_r$ that satisfies (2.10) by showing that all polynomials $\phi_{S_1((\lambda - \alpha)\beta^{-1})}$ belong to a certain linear space $L \in \mathbb{F}_r[x]/(x^p - 1)$ of dimension less than p. In this case any (nonzero) map $T : \mathbb{F}_p \to \mathbb{F}_r$ such that $\phi_T \in L^\perp$ can be used as the map S_0.

Let

$$\tau(x) = \gcd(x^p - 1, \phi_{S_1}(x)).$$

Note that $\tau(x) \neq 1$, since g is a common root of $x^p - 1$ and $\phi_{S_1}(x)$. Let L be the space of polynomials in $\mathbb{F}_r[x]/(x^p - 1)$ that are multiples of $\tau(x)$. Clearly, $\dim L = p - \deg \tau$. Fix some $\alpha \in \mathbb{F}_p$ and $\beta \in \langle r \rangle$. Let us prove that $\phi_{S_1((\lambda - \alpha)\beta^{-1})}(x)$ is in L:

$$\phi_{S_1((\lambda-\alpha)\beta^{-1})}(x) = x^\alpha \phi_{S_1}(x^\beta) = x^\alpha (\phi_{S_1}(x))^\beta.$$

The last identity above follows from the fact that for any $f \in \mathbb{F}_r[x]$ and any positive integer i,

$$f\left(x^{r^i}\right) = (f(x))^{r^i}.$$

This completes the proof.   □

Lemma 8 reduces the task of proving the k-algebraic niceness of $\langle r \rangle \subseteq \mathbb{F}_p^*$ to certifying the existence of a nontrivial k-dependence in C_r^p. In the following subsections, we present several sufficient conditions for the existence of such a dependence.

Our first sufficient condition (Lemma 9) is the following: p is a Mersenne prime and $r = 2$. The proof that this condition suffices is simple and self-contained. This result alone yields most of our improvements for binary locally decodable codes (see Lemma 14 and Section 2.7.1). Two weaker sufficient conditions are given in Lemmas 10 and 13. Those lemmas have fairly technical proofs and are used later to obtain the most general form of our results for locally decodable codes (see Section 2.7.2).

2.6.1 3-dependences between p-th roots: sufficient conditions

Lemma 9. *Suppose that $p = 2^t - 1$ is a Mersenne prime; then there exists a nontrivial three-dependence in C_2^p.*

Proof. Observe that the polynomial

$$x^p - 1 = x^{2^t-1} - 1 \in \mathbb{F}_2[x]$$

splits into distinct linear factors in the finite field $\mathbb{F}_{2^t}$. Therefore $C_2^p = \mathbb{F}_{2^t}^*$. Pick $\zeta_1 \neq \zeta_2$ in C_2^p arbitrarily. Set $\zeta_3 = \zeta_1 + \zeta_2$. Note that $\zeta_3 \in C_2^p$ and

$$\zeta_1 + \zeta_2 + \zeta_3 = 0.$$

This completes the proof.   □

Now we generalize Lemma 9 and show that a substantially weaker condition on p and r is still sufficient. Our argument relies on the classical Weil bound [62, p. 330] for the number of rational points on curves over finite fields.

Lemma 10. *Let p and r be distinct primes. Suppose that $\mathrm{ord}_p(r) < (4/3)\log_r p$; then there exists a nontrivial three-dependence in C_r^p.*

Proof. We start with a brief review of some basic concepts of projective algebraic geometry [29]. Let $\mathbb{F}$ be a field, and let $f \in \mathbb{F}[x,y,z]$ be a homogeneous polynomial. A triple $(x_0, y_0, z_0) \in \mathbb{F}^3$ is called a zero of f if $f(x_0, y_0, z_0) = 0$. A zero is called "nontrivial" if it is different from the origin. An equation $f = 0$ defines a projective plane curve χ_f. Nontrivial zeros of f, considered up to multiplication by a scalar, are called $\mathbb{F}$-rational points of χ_f. If $\mathbb{F}$ is a finite field, it makes sense to talk about the number of $\mathbb{F}$-rational points on a curve.

Let $t = \mathrm{ord}_p(r)$. Note that $C_r^p \subseteq \mathbb{F}_{r^t}$. Pick $\{\sigma_i\}_{i \in [3]}$ in $\mathbb{F}_r^*$ such that

$$\sigma_1 + \sigma_2 + \sigma_3 \neq 0.$$

Consider a projective plane curve χ defined by

$$\sigma_1 x^{(r^t-1)/p} + \sigma_2 y^{(r^t-1)/p} + \sigma_3 z^{(r^t-1)/p} = 0. \tag{2.11}$$

Let us call a point $\mathbf{a}$ on χ "trivial" if one of the coordinates of $\mathbf{a}$ is zero. Clearly, there are at most $3(r^t - 1)/p$ trivial points on χ. Note that every nontrivial $\mathbb{F}_{r^t}$-rational point of χ yields a nontrivial 3-dependence in C_r^p (since $\mathbb{F}_{r^t}^*$ is cyclic). The classical Weil bound [62, p. 330] provides an estimate

$$\left| N_q - (q+1) \right| \leq (d-1)(d-2)\sqrt{q} \tag{2.12}$$

for the number N_q of $\mathbb{F}_q$-rational points on an arbitrary smooth projective plane curve of degree d. Equation (2.12) implies that if

$$r^t + 1 > \left(\frac{r^t - 1}{p} - 1 \right) \left(\frac{r^t - 1}{p} - 2 \right) r^{t/2} + 3 \frac{r^t - 1}{p} \tag{2.13}$$

there exists a nontrivial point on the curve (2.11). Note that (2.13) follows from

$$r^t + 1 > \left(\frac{r^t}{p} \right) \left(\frac{r^t}{p} \right) r^{t/2} - \frac{2r^{3t/2}}{p} + \frac{3r^t}{p}, \tag{2.14}$$

and (2.14) follows from

$$r^t > \frac{r^{2t+t/2}}{p^2} \quad \text{and} \quad 2r^{t/2} > 3.$$

Now note that the first inequality above follows from $t < (4/3)\log_r p$. To prove the second inequality, observe that $r \geq 3$ implies $2r^{1/2} > 3$, and $r = 2$ implies $t \geq 2$. $\quad\square$

2.6.2 k-dependences between p-th roots: a sufficient condition

In this section, we show that one can relax the conditions of Lemma 10 further and still ensure the existence of nontrivial k-dependences in C_r^p (for $k \geq 3$). Our proof is quite technical and comes in three steps. First, we briefly review the notion of (additive) Fourier coefficients of subsets of $\mathbb{F}_{r^t}$. Next, we invoke a folklore argument to show that subsets of $\mathbb{F}_{r^t}$ with appropriately small nontrivial Fourier coefficients contain nontrivial k-dependences. Finally, we use a recent result of Bourgain and

Chang [23] (which generalizes the classical estimate for Gauss sums) to argue that (under certain constraints on p and r) all nontrivial Fourier coefficients of C_r^p are small.

For a prime r, let $\mathbb{C}_r$ denote the multiplicative group of complex r-th roots of unity. Let $e \in \mathbb{C}_r$ be an r-th root other than the identity. For $x \in \mathbb{F}_{r^t}$, let

$$\mathrm{Tr}(x) = x + x^r + \ldots + x^{r^{t-1}}$$

denote the trace of x. It is not hard to verify that for all x, $\mathrm{Tr}(x) \in \mathbb{F}_r$. The characters of $\mathbb{F}_{r^t}$ are homomorphisms from the additive group of $\mathbb{F}_{r^t}$ into $\mathbb{C}_r$. There exist r^t characters. We denote the characters by χ_a, where a ranges over $\mathbb{F}_{r^t}$, and set

$$\chi_a(x) = e^{\mathrm{Tr}(ax)}.$$

Let $C(x)$ denote the incidence function of a set $C \subseteq \mathbb{F}_{r^t}$. For arbitrary $a \in \mathbb{F}_{r^t}$, the Fourier coefficient $\hat{C}(\chi_a)$ is defined by

$$\hat{C}(\chi_a) = \sum \chi_a(x)C(x),$$

where the sum is over all $x \in \mathbb{F}_{r^t}$. The Fourier coefficient $\hat{C}(\chi_0) = |C|$ is said to be *trivial*, and the other Fourier coefficients are said to be *nontrivial*. In what follows, $\sum_a$ stands for summation over all r^t elements of $\mathbb{F}_{r^t}$. We need the following two standard properties of characters and Fourier coefficients:

$$\sum_a \chi_a(x) = \begin{cases} r^t, & \text{if } x = 0, \\ 0, & \text{otherwise,} \end{cases} \tag{2.15}$$

$$\sum_a \left| \hat{C}(\chi_a) \right|^2 = r^t |C|. \tag{2.16}$$

The following lemma is part of mathematical folklore.

Lemma 11. *Let $C \subseteq \mathbb{F}_{r^t}$ and let $k \geq 3$ be an integer such that there exist $\{\sigma_i\}_{i \in [k]}$ in $\mathbb{F}_r^*$, where $\sum_{i \in [k]} \sigma_i \neq 0$. Let F be the largest absolute value of a nontrivial Fourier coefficient of C. Suppose that*

$$\frac{F}{|C|} < \left(\frac{|C|}{r^t} \right)^{1/(k-2)}; \tag{2.17}$$

then there exists a nontrivial k-dependence between the elements of C.

Proof. Let
$$M(C) = \#\{\zeta_1, \ldots, \zeta_k \in C \mid \sigma_1\zeta_1 + \ldots + \sigma_k\zeta_k = 0\}.$$

The identity (2.15) yields

$$M(C) = \frac{1}{r^t} \sum_{x_1, \ldots, x_k \in \mathbb{F}_{r^t}} C(x_1) \ldots C(x_k) \sum_a \chi_a(\sigma_1 x_1 + \ldots + \sigma_k x_k). \tag{2.18}$$

Note that
$$\chi_a(\sigma_1 x_1 + \ldots + \sigma_k x_k) = \chi_{\sigma_1 a}(x_1) \ldots \chi_{\sigma_k a}(x_k).$$

Changing the order of summation in (2.18), we get

$$M(C) = \frac{1}{r^t} \sum_a \sum_{x_1,\ldots,x_k \in \mathbb{F}_{r^t}} C(x_1)\ldots C(x_k)\chi_{\sigma_1 a}(x_1)\ldots\chi_{\sigma_k a}(x_k). \tag{2.19}$$

Separating the term corresponding to $a = 0$ in the right-hand side of (2.19), we get

$$M(C) = \frac{|C|^k}{r^t} + \frac{1}{r^t}\sum_{a\neq 0}\prod_{i=1}^{k}\hat{C}(\chi_{\sigma_i a}) \geq \frac{|C|^k}{r^t} - \frac{1}{r^t}\sum_{a\neq 0}\prod_{i=1}^{k}|\hat{C}(\chi_{\sigma_i a})|. \tag{2.20}$$

Using the generalized Holder's inequality [13, p. 20], we obtain

$$\sum_{a\neq 0}\prod_{i=1}^{k}|\hat{C}(\chi_{\sigma_i a})| \leq \prod_{i=1}^{k}\left(\sum_{a\neq 0}|\hat{C}(\chi_{\sigma_i a})|^k\right)^{1/k}. \tag{2.21}$$

Note that for every $i \in [k]$ we have

$$\sum_{a\neq 0}|\hat{C}(\chi_{\sigma_i a})|^k \leq F^{k-2}\sum_{a}|\hat{C}(\chi_{\sigma_i a})|^2 = F^{k-2}r^t|C|, \tag{2.22}$$

where the last identity follows from (2.16). Combining (2.20), (2.21), and (2.22) we get

$$M(C) \geq \frac{|C|^k}{r^t} - F^{k-2}|C|, \tag{2.23}$$

and conclude that (2.17) implies $M(C) > 0$. $\qquad\square$

The following lemma is due to Bourgain and Chang [23, Theorem 1].

Lemma 12. *Assume that $n \mid r^t - 1$ and satisfies the condition*

$$\gcd\left(n, \frac{r^t - 1}{r^{t'} - 1}\right) < r^{t(1-\varepsilon)-t'} \quad \text{for all} \ \ 1 \leq t' < t, \ t' \mid t,$$

where $\varepsilon > 0$ is arbitrary and fixed. Then, for all $a \in \mathbb{F}_{r^t}^*$,

$$\left|\sum_{x\in\mathbb{F}_{r^t}} e^{\mathrm{Tr}(ax^n)}\right| < c_1 r^{t(1-\delta)}, \tag{2.24}$$

where $\delta = \delta(\varepsilon) > 0$ and $c_1 = c_1(\varepsilon)$ are constants.

The main result of this subsection is presented below. Recall that C_r^p denotes the set of p-th roots of unity in $\overline{\mathbb{F}}_r$.

Lemma 13. *For every $c > 0$ and prime r, there exists an integer $k = k(c,r)$ such that the following implication holds. If $p \neq r$ is a prime and $\mathrm{ord}_p(r) < c \log_r p$, then there is a nontrivial k-dependence between the elements of C_r^p.*

Proof. Note that the sum of all p-th roots of unity in $\overline{\mathbb{F}}_r$ is zero. Therefore, given r and c, it suffices to prove the existence of a $k = k(c,r)$ that works for all *sufficiently large* p.

Let $t = \mathrm{ord}_p(r)$. Observe that $p > r^{t/c}$. Assume that p is sufficiently large that $t > 2c$. We now show that the precondition of Lemma 12 holds for $n = (r^t - 1)/p$ and $\varepsilon = 1/(2c)$. Let $t' \mid t$ and $1 \leq t' < t$. Clearly, $\gcd(r^{t'} - 1, p) = 1$. Therefore

$$\gcd\left(\frac{r^t - 1}{p}, \frac{r^t - 1}{r^{t'} - 1}\right) = \frac{r^t - 1}{p(r^{t'} - 1)} < \frac{r^{t(1-1/c)}}{r^{t'} - 1}, \tag{2.25}$$

where the inequality follows from $p > r^{t/c}$. Clearly, $t > 2c$ yields $r^{t/(2c)}/2 > 1$. Multiplying the right-hand side of (2.25) by $r^{t/(2c)}/2$ and using $2(r^{t'} - 1) \geq r^{t'}$, we get

$$\gcd\left(\frac{r^t - 1}{p}, \frac{r^t - 1}{r^{t'} - 1}\right) < r^{t(1-1/(2c))-t'}. \tag{2.26}$$

Combining (2.26) with Lemma 12, we conclude that there exist $\delta > 0$ and c_1 such that for all $a \in \mathbb{F}_{r^t}^*$,

$$\left| \sum_{x \in \mathbb{F}_{r^t}} e^{\mathrm{Tr}\left(ax^{(r^t-1)/p}\right)} \right| < c_1 r^{t(1-\delta)}. \tag{2.27}$$

Observe that $x^{(r^t-1)/p}$ takes every value in C_r^p exactly $(r^t - 1)/p$ times when x ranges over $\mathbb{F}_{r^t}^*$. Thus (2.27) implies

$$(r^t - 1)\left(\frac{F}{p}\right) < c_1 r^{t(1-\delta)} + 1, \tag{2.28}$$

where F denotes the largest absolute value of a nontrivial Fourier coefficient of C_r^p. Assuming that t is sufficiently large, we get

$$(r^t - 1)\left(\frac{F}{p}\right) < c_2 r^{t(1-\delta)}, \tag{2.29}$$

for a suitably chosen constant c_2. Equation (2.29) yields $F/p < (2c_2)r^{-\delta t}$. Pick $k \geq 3$ to be an *odd* integer large enough so that $(1 - 1/c)/(k - 2) < \delta$. We now have

$$\frac{F}{p} < r^{-\frac{(1-1/c)t}{(k-2)}} \tag{2.30}$$

for all sufficiently large values of p. Combining $p > r^{t/c}$ with (2.30), we get

$$\frac{F}{|C_r^p|} < \left(\frac{|C_r^p|}{r^t}\right)^{1/(k-2)},$$

and an application of Lemma 11 together with the observation that for odd k there always exist $\{\sigma_i\}_{i\in[k]}$ in $\mathbb{F}_r^*$, where $\sum_{i\in[k]}\sigma_i \neq 0$, conclude the proof. $\qquad\square$

2.6.3 Summary

We now summarize our sufficient conditions on p and r that yield algebraic niceness of $\langle r \rangle \subseteq \mathbb{F}_p^*$ over $\mathbb{F}_r$. Combining Lemmas 8 and 9 we get the following.

Lemma 14. *Suppose that $p = 2^t - 1$ is a Mersenne prime; then $\langle 2 \rangle \subseteq \mathbb{F}_p^*$ is three-algebraically nice over $\mathbb{F}_2$.*

Using Lemma 10 instead of Lemma 9 (in combination with Lemma 8) we get a weaker sufficient condition.

Lemma 15. *Suppose that p and r are distinct primes such that $\mathrm{ord}_p(r) \leq (4/3)\log_r p$; then $\langle r \rangle \subseteq \mathbb{F}_p^*$ is three-algebraically nice over $\mathbb{F}_r$.*

Finally, combining Lemmas 8 and 13 we get the following.

Lemma 16. *For every $c > 0$ and prime r there exists an integer $k = k(c,r)$ such that the following implication holds. If $p \neq r$ is a prime and $\mathrm{ord}_p(r) < c\log_r p$, then $\langle r \rangle \subseteq \mathbb{F}_p^*$ is k-algebraically nice over $\mathbb{F}_r$.*

2.7 Results

In what follows, we put the results of the previous sections together and summarize our improvements in upper bounds for the codeword length of locally decodable codes.

In Section 2.7.1, we present our results for the narrow case of three-query binary codes. First we show that given a single Mersenne prime $p = 2^t - 1$, one can design three-query binary LDCs of length $\exp\left(n^{1/t}\right)$ for every message length n. Next we review the achievements of the centuries-old study of Mersenne primes, and obtain new families of locally decodable codes that yield large improvements upon earlier work.

In Section 2.7.2, we present the general form of our results. We show that if r is a prime and $r^t - 1$ has a polynomially large prime factor $p \geq r^{\gamma t}$, then for every message length n there exists a $k(\gamma)$-query r-ary LDC of length $\exp\left(n^{1/t}\right)$. The query complexity of the codes that we obtain depends on the size of the largest prime factor of $r^t - 1$, and the codeword length depends on the size of $r^t - 1$ itself. The larger the largest prime factor is, the smaller is the query complexity. The larger $r^t - 1$ is the shorter are the codes.

2.7.1 Results for three-query binary codes

By combining proposition 4 with Lemmas 7 and 14, we conclude that every Mersenne prime $p = 2^t - 1$ yields a family of 3-query locally decodable codes of length $\exp\left(n^{1/t}\right)$.

Theorem 2. *Suppose that $p = 2^t - 1$ is a Mersenne prime; then for every message length n, there exists a binary linear code of length $\exp\left(n^{1/t}\right)$ that is $(3, \delta, 6\delta)$-locally decodable for all δ.*

Mersenne primes have been a popular object of study in number theory for the last few centuries. The largest known Mersenne prime (as of June 2007) is $p = 2^{32\,582\,657} - 1$. It was discovered by Cooper and Boone [1] on September 4, 2006. Plugging p into Theorem 2, we get the following theorem.

Theorem 3. *For every message length n there exists a binary linear code of length $\exp\left(n^{1/32\,582\,657}\right)$ that is $(3, \delta, 6\delta)$-locally decodable for all δ.*

It has often been conjectured that the number of Mersenne primes is infinite. If this conjecture holds, we get three-query locally decodable codes of subexponential length *for infinitely many* message lengths n. To prove this, we first combine Proposition 3 with Lemmas 6 and 14 to obtain the following lemma.

Lemma 17. *Let $p = 2^t - 1$ be a Mersenne prime and let $m \geq p - 1$ be an integer. Let $m' = \binom{m-1+(p-1)/t}{(p-1)/t}$. There exists a binary linear code encoding $n = \binom{m}{p-1}$-bit messages to $p^{m'}$-bit codewords that is $(3, \delta, 6\delta)$-locally decodable code for all δ.*

Now we proceed to constructing a family of three-query binary LDCs of subexponential length.

Theorem 4. *Suppose that the number of Mersenne primes is infinite; then for infinitely many values of the message length n, there exists a binary linear code of length $\exp\left(n^{O(1/\log\log n)}\right)$ that is $(3, \delta, 6\delta)$-locally decodable for all δ.*

Proof. Given a Mersenne prime p, set $m = 2^p$. By substituting m and p into Lemma 17 and doing some basic manipulations, we conclude that there exists a $(3, \delta, 6\delta)$-locally decodable code encoding $n = m^{\Theta(\log m)}$ bits to

$$N = \exp\left(m^{O(\log m/\log\log m)}\right)$$

bits. An observation that $\log\log n = \Theta(\log\log m)$ completes the proof. $\square$

Lenstra, Pomerance, and Wagstaff [2, 74, 90] have made the following conjecture regarding the density of Mersenne primes.

Conjecture 1. Let $M(t)$ be the number of Mersenne primes that are less than or equal to $2^t - 1$; then

$$\lim_{t \to \infty} \frac{M(t)}{\log_2 t} = e^\gamma,$$

where $\gamma \approx 0.577$ is the Euler–Mascheroni constant.

If this conjecture holds, we get three-query locally decodable codes of subexponential length *for all* message lengths n.

Theorem 5. *Let ε be a positive constant. Suppose that conjecture 1 holds; then for every message length n, there exists a binary linear code of length* exp $\left(n^{O\left(1/\log^{1-\varepsilon}\log n\right)}\right)$ *that is* $(3, \delta, 6\delta)$ *locally decodable for all δ.*

Proof. Conjecture 1 implies that for all sufficiently large integers z, there is a Mersenne prime between $2^{\log^{1-\varepsilon} z}$ and z. Assume that n is sufficiently large. Pick a Mersenne prime p from the interval

$$\left[2^{\log^{1-\varepsilon} \sqrt{\log n}}, \sqrt{\log n} \right].$$

Let m be the smallest integer such that $n \leq \binom{m}{p-1}$. Note that $m = pn^{\Theta(1/p)}$. Given an n-bit message x, we pad it with zeros to a length $\binom{m}{p-1}$ and use the code in Lemma 17 to encode x into a codeword of length $p^{m'}$ for

$$m' = \left(n^{1/p} \log p \right)^{O(p/\log p)}.$$

It remains to note that

$$\log m' = O\left(\frac{\log n}{\log p} + \frac{p \log \log p}{\log p} \right) = O\left(\frac{\log n}{\log^{1-\varepsilon} \log n} \right).$$

This completes the proof. $\qquad\qquad\qquad\qquad\qquad\qquad\qquad\qquad\qquad\qquad\square$

2.7.2 Results for general codes

For an integer m, let $P(m)$ denote the largest prime factor of m. Our first theorem gets three-query r-ary LDCs from numbers $m = r^t - 1$ such that $P(m) > m^{3/4}$.

Theorem 6. *Let r be a prime. Suppose that $P(r^t - 1) > r^{0.75t}$; then for every message length n, there exists a three-query r-ary code of length* exp $\left(n^{1/t}\right)$ *that is* $(3, \delta, 3\delta r/(r-1))$-*locally decodable for all δ.*

Proof. Let $P(r^t - 1) = p$. Observe that $p \mid r^t - 1$ and $p > r^{0.75t}$ yield

$$\mathrm{ord}_p(r) < (4/3) \log_r p.$$

By combining Lemmas 15 and 7 with Proposition 4, we obtain the statement of the theorem. $\qquad\qquad\qquad\qquad\qquad\qquad\qquad\qquad\qquad\qquad\square$

As an example application of theorem 6, one can observe that

$$P(2^{23} - 1) = 178\,481 > 2^{(3/4)*23} \approx 155\,872$$

yields a family of three-query locally decodable codes of length $\exp(n^{1/23})$. Theorem 6 immediately yields the following theorem.

Theorem 7. *Let r be a prime. Suppose, for infinitely many t, we have $P(r^t - 1) > r^{0.75t}$; then for every $\varepsilon > 0$ and for every message length n, there exists a three-query r-ary code of length $\exp(n^\varepsilon)$ that is $(3, \delta, 3\delta r/(r-1))$-locally decodable for all δ.*

The next theorem gets constant-query LDCs from numbers $m = r^t - 1$ with prime factors larger than m^γ for every value of γ.

Theorem 8. *Let r be a prime. For every $\gamma > 0$, there exists an integer $k = k(\gamma, r)$ such that the following implication holds. Suppose that $P(r^t - 1) > r^{\gamma t}$; then for every message length n, there exists a k-query r-ary code of length $\exp(n^{1/t})$ that is $(k, \delta, \delta k r/(r-1))$-locally decodable for all δ.*

Proof. Let $P(r^t - 1) = p$. Observe that $p \mid r^t - 1$ and $p > r^{\gamma t}$ yield

$$\mathrm{ord}_p(r) < (1/\gamma) \log_r p.$$

By combining Lemmas 16 and 7 with Proposition 4, we obtain the statement of the theorem.   □

As an immediate corollary, we get the following.

Theorem 9. *Let r be a prime. Suppose, for some $\gamma > 0$ and infinitely many t, we have $P(r^t - 1) > r^{\gamma t}$; then there is a fixed k such that for every $\varepsilon > 0$ and every message length n, there exists a k-query r-ary code of length $\exp(n^\varepsilon)$ that is $(k, \delta, \delta k r/(r-1))$-locally decodable for all δ.*

2.8 Addendum

The locally decodable codes of the third generation that were introduced in this book have been developed further in [20, 36, 38, 55, 75]. Specifically,

- Raghavendra [75] suggested an alternative conceptually simpler framework for viewing the construction. The key observation underlying Raghavendra's view is that the maps S_0 and S_1 in the definition of algebraic niceness (Definition 7) can be fixed in a certain canonical form.
- Using Raghavendra's view, Efremenko [38] generalized the construction to work over composites; i.e., Efremenko replaced the field $\mathbb{F}_q$ by a ring $\mathbb{Z}_b$ for a composite b in Definitions 6, 5, and 7. Efremenko used a powerful result of Grolmusz [49] showing that certain subsets of $\mathbb{Z}_b$ are combinatorially far "nicer" than any subsets of $\mathbb{F}_q$, and obtained substantial improvements in upper bounds for the codeword length.
- Finally, Dvir et al. [36] suggested yet another view of the construction. They also studied code parameters in the regime of super-constant query complexity.

In order to demonstrate the key ideas behind the follow-up work, below we review the construction of LDCs of the third generation following the (most recent) view of Dvir et al. [36].

This view fleshes out an intrinsic similarity between locally decodable codes of the third generation and classical Reed–Muller codes. An r-ary locally decodable code consists of a linear subspace of polynomials in $\mathbb{F}_r[z_1, \ldots, z_m]$, evaluated at all points of

$$C_b^m = C_b \times \ldots \times C_b \quad (m \text{ times}),$$

where C_b is a certain multiplicative subgroup of $\mathbb{F}_r^*$.

The decoding algorithm is similar to the traditional local decoders for Reed–Muller codes. The decoder shoots a line in a certain direction and decodes along it (see the locally decodable code described in Section 1.1). The difference is that the monomials which are used are not of low degree; instead, they are chosen according to a *matching* family of vectors (see the following definition). Further, the lines for decoding are *multiplicative*, a notion that we will define shortly.

Definition 9. Let b be an arbitrary positive integer. We say that the families $\mathscr{U} = \{\mathbf{u}_1, \ldots, \mathbf{u}_n\}$ and $\mathscr{V} = \{\mathbf{v}_1, \ldots, \mathbf{v}_n\}$ of vectors in $\mathbb{Z}_b^m$ form a matching family if the following two conditions are satisfied:

- For all $i \in [n]$, $(\mathbf{u}_i, \mathbf{v}_i) = 0$.
- For all $i, j \in [n]$ such that $i \neq j$, $(\mathbf{u}_j, \mathbf{v}_i) \neq 0$.

Observe that the concept of a matching family is intimately related to the concept of combinatorial niceness of a set (Definition 3). We now show how one can obtain a locally decodable code out of a matching family of vectors. We start with some notation.

- A D-evaluation of a function f defined over a domain D is a vector of values of f at all points of D.
- Let $\mathbf{w} \in \mathbb{Z}_b^m$ be a vector and let $l \in [m]$ be an integer. In this section, we write $\mathbf{w}(l)$ to denote the l-th coordinate of $\mathbf{w}$.
- We assume that r is a prime power and that b divides $r - 1$; we denote a multiplicative subgroup of $\mathbb{F}_r^*$ of order b by C_b.
- We fix some generator g of C_b.
- For $\mathbf{w} \in \mathbb{Z}_b^m$, we define $g^{\mathbf{w}} \in C_b^m$ by $\left(g^{\mathbf{w}(1)}, \ldots, g^{\mathbf{w}(m)}\right)$.
- For $\mathbf{w}, \mathbf{v} \in \mathbb{Z}_b^m$ we define the multiplicative line $M_{\mathbf{w}, \mathbf{v}}$ through $\mathbf{w}$ in the direction $\mathbf{v}$ to be the multiset

$$M_{\mathbf{w}, \mathbf{v}} = \left\{ g^{\mathbf{w} + \lambda \mathbf{v}} \mid \lambda \in \mathbb{Z}_b \right\}. \tag{2.31}$$

- For $\mathbf{u} \in \mathbb{Z}_b^m$, we define the monomial $\mathrm{mon}_{\mathbf{u}} \in \mathbb{F}_r[z_1, \ldots, z_m]$ by

$$\mathrm{mon}_{\mathbf{u}}(z_1, \ldots, z_m) = \prod_{l \in [m]} z_l^{\mathbf{u}(l)}. \tag{2.32}$$

Note that for any $\mathbf{w}, \mathbf{u}, \mathbf{v} \in \mathbb{Z}_b^m$ and $\lambda \in \mathbb{Z}_b$ we have

$$\text{mon}_{\mathbf{u}}\left(g^{\mathbf{w}+\lambda\mathbf{v}}\right) = g^{(\mathbf{u},\mathbf{w})}\left(g^{\lambda}\right)^{(\mathbf{u},\mathbf{v})}. \tag{2.33}$$

The formula above implies that the $M_{\mathbf{w},\mathbf{v}}$-evaluation of a monomial $\text{mon}_{\mathbf{u}}$ is a C_b-evaluation of a (univariate) monomial

$$g^{(\mathbf{u},\mathbf{w})}y^{(\mathbf{u},\mathbf{v})} \in \mathbb{F}_r[y]. \tag{2.34}$$

This observation is the foundation of the decoding algorithm. We are now ready to formally specify the locally decodable code.

2.8.1 The code

Proposition 5. *Let $\mathscr{U}, \mathscr{V}$ be a family of matching vectors in $\mathbb{Z}_b^m$, $|\mathscr{U}| = |\mathscr{V}| = n$. Suppose that $b \mid r - 1$, where r is a prime power; then there exists an r-ary linear code encoding messages of length n to codewords of length b^m that is $(b, \delta, b\delta)$-locally decodable for all δ.*

Proof. We specify the encoding and decoding procedures for our code as follows.

Encoding. We encode a message $(\mathbf{x}(1), \ldots, \mathbf{x}(n)) \in \mathbb{F}_r^n$ by the C_b^m-evaluation of the polynomial

$$F(z_1, \ldots, z_m) = \sum_{j=1}^{n} \mathbf{x}(j) \times \text{mon}_{\mathbf{u}_j}(z_1, \ldots, z_m). \tag{2.35}$$

Decoding. The input to the decoder is a (corrupted) C_b^m-evaluation of F and an index $i \in [n]$. To recover the value $\mathbf{x}(i)$, the decoder picks $\mathbf{w} \in \mathbb{Z}_b^m$ at random, and queries the (possibly corrupted) $M_{\mathbf{w},\mathbf{v}_i}$-evaluation of F at all b points.

We now claim that the noiseless $M_{\mathbf{w},\mathbf{v}_i}$-evaluation of F uniquely determines $\mathbf{x}(i)$. To see this, note that by (2.33), (2.34), and (2.35), the $M_{\mathbf{w},\mathbf{v}_i}$-evaluation of F is a C_b-evaluation of a polynomial

$$f(y) = \sum_{j=1}^{n} \mathbf{x}(j) \times g^{(\mathbf{u}_j,\mathbf{w})}y^{(\mathbf{u}_j,\mathbf{v}_i)} \in \mathbb{F}_r[y]. \tag{2.36}$$

We observe further that the properties of the matching family $\mathscr{U}, \mathscr{V}$ and (2.36) yield

$$f(y) = \mathbf{x}(i) \times g^{(\mathbf{u}_i,\mathbf{w})} + \sum_{s \in \mathbb{Z}_b \setminus \{0\}} \left(\sum_{j \,:\, (\mathbf{u}_j,\mathbf{v}_i)=s} \mathbf{x}(j) \times g^{(\mathbf{u}_j,\mathbf{w})} \right) y^s. \tag{2.37}$$

It is evident from the above formula that

$$\mathbf{x}(i) = f(0)/g^{(\mathbf{u}_i,\mathbf{w})}. \tag{2.38}$$

Therefore all the decoder needs to do is recover the unique univariate polynomial $f(y) \in \mathbb{F}_r[y]$, of degree up to $r - 1$, whose C_b-evaluation agrees with the (observed) $M_{\mathbf{w},\mathbf{v}_i}$-evaluation of F, and return $f(0)/g^{(\mathbf{u}_i,\mathbf{w})}$.

To estimate the probability of a decoding error, we note that each individual query of the decoder goes to a uniformly random location, and apply the union bound. $\square$

By applying Proposition 5 to the currently largest known family of matching vectors [49], one gets the locally decodable codes of [38].

Chapter 3
Limitations of the point removal method

In the previous chapter, we gave a detailed exposition of the point removal method for constructing locally decodable codes and obtained large improvements upon earlier work. Our most general result (Theorem 8) said that if r is a prime and $r^t - 1$ has a polynomially large prime factor $p \geq r^\eta$, then there exists a family of $k(\gamma)$-query r-ary LDCs of length $\exp\left(n^{1/t}\right)$.

In this chapter, we prove a partial converse of Theorem 8. Namely, we show that if, for some fixed k and all $\varepsilon > 0$, one can use the point removal method over finite fields to obtain a family of r-ary k-query codes of length $\exp\left(n^\varepsilon\right)$, then infinitely many numbers of the form $r^t - 1$ have prime factors larger than those known currently. Our result identifies the problem of establishing strong lower bounds on the size of the largest prime factors of (Mersenne-type) numbers $r^t - 1$ as the current barrier to further progress on LDC constructions via the point removal method.

3.1 Attaining subexponential length requires a nice sequence

We start with a high-level review of our construction of locally decodable codes via point removal that was given earlier in Chapter 2.

3.1.1 Point removal method

There were two steps in the construction. First, in Propositions 3 and 4, we argued that every subset S of a finite field $\mathbb{F}_q$ that exhibits two properties (namely, t-combinatorial niceness and k-algebraic niceness) yields a family of k-query locally decodable codes of length $\exp\left(n^{1/t}\right)$. Next, we came up with a specific set that is simultaneously combinatorially and algebraically nice. Let $P(m)$ denote the largest prime factor of an integer m. In Lemmas 7 and 16, we argued that for a prime r such

S. Yekhanin, *Locally Decodable Codes and Private Information Retrieval Schemes*,
Information Security and Cryptography, DOI 10.1007/978-3-642-14358-8_3,
© Springer-Verlag Berlin Heidelberg 2010

that $p = P(r^t - 1) \geq r^{\gamma t}$, the multiplicative subgroup of $\mathbb{F}_p^*$ generated by r (which we denote by $\langle r \rangle$) is simultaneously t-combinatorially nice and $k(\gamma)$-algebraically nice.

A combination of the two steps above led to Theorems 6 and 8, saying that every number of the form $r^t - 1$ that has a polynomially large prime factor gives rise to a family of short locally decodable codes. By instantiating Theorem 6 with the largest known Mersenne prime, we got three-query binary codes of length $\exp\left(n^{1/32\,582\,657}\right)$, presenting a large improvement upon earlier work.

3.1.2 Point removal and bounds for $P(r^t - 1)$

Given the magnitude of our improvements, it is natural to ask if the same technique could lead to even shorter codes. Specifically, one could ask whether it is possible to use the same ideas to obtain families of k-query codes of length $\exp(n^\varepsilon)$ for some fixed k and all $\varepsilon > 0$.

In Theorems 7 and 9 we identified a number-theoretic claim that we need in order to get such codes via the sets $\langle r \rangle \subseteq \mathbb{F}_p^*$. Specifically, we argued that we need a theorem saying that for some $\gamma > 0$ and for some prime r, there exist infinitely many t such that

$$P(r^t - 1) \geq r^{\gamma t}.$$

However, proving such a strong lower bound on the size of the largest prime factors of Mersenne-type numbers is far beyond what number theorists can do today. Lower bounds for $P(r^t - 1)$ have received a considerable amount of attention, especially in the case of $r = 2$ [39, 41, 67, 68, 82, 84, 85]. The strongest result to date is due to Stewart [85]. This says that for all integers t, ignoring a set of asymptotic density zero, and for all functions $\varepsilon(t) > 0$ where $\varepsilon(t)$ tends to zero monotonically and arbitrarily slowly,

$$P(2^t - 1) > \frac{\varepsilon(t)t\,(\log t)^2}{\log\log t}. \tag{3.1}$$

Although the bound (3.1) may seem extremely weak in light of the conjecture saying that the number of Mersenne primes is infinite, there are no better bounds known to hold for infinitely many values of t, unless one is willing to accept some number-theoretic conjectures [67, 68].

3.1.3 Our results

In this chapter, we show that the need for stronger lower bounds for $P(r^t - 1)$ does not arise because of a poor choice of the set $S = \langle r \rangle \subseteq \mathbb{F}_p^*$ but, rather, is essential to the whole point removal method. Specifically, we show that if, for some prime r, constant k, and every $\varepsilon > 0$, one can pick a finite field $\mathbb{F}$ and a set $S \subseteq \mathbb{F}^*$ to (unconditionally) obtain a family of k-query LDCs of length $\exp(n^\varepsilon)$ via Proposition 4, then for infinitely many t we have

$$P(r^t - 1) \geq \left(\frac{t}{2}\right)^{1+1/(k-2)}. \tag{3.2}$$

To get a feeling for whether the bound above represents a serious barrier to further progress on upper bounds for locally decodable codes via point removal, note that in the case $r = 2$ the bound (3.2) is substantially stronger than what is currently known unconditionally (3.1) (for any $k \geq 3$).

We now introduce the notion of a k-nice sequence of subsets of finite fields.

Definition 10. Let r be a prime. We say that a sequence

$$\left\{ S_i \subseteq \mathbb{F}_{q_i}^* \right\}_{i \geq 1}$$

of subsets of finite fields is k-nice over $\mathbb{F}_r$ if every S_i is k-algebraically nice over $\mathbb{F}_r$ and $t(i)$-combinatorially nice, for some integer-valued monotonically increasing function t.

It is easy to verify that one needs to exhibit a sequence that is k-nice over $\mathbb{F}_r$ in order to obtain k-query r-ary locally decodable codes of length $\exp(n^\varepsilon)$ for some fixed k and every $\varepsilon > 0$ via Proposition 4.

In what follows, we show how the existence of a k-nice sequence over $\mathbb{F}_r$ implies that infinitely many numbers $r^t - 1$ have large prime factors. Recall that C_r^p denotes the set of p-th roots of unity in $\overline{\mathbb{F}}_r$. Recall also our notion of a *nontrivial k-dependence:* there is a nontrivial k-dependence in C_r^p if there exist $\{\zeta_i\}_{i \in [k]} \subseteq C_r^p$ and $\{\sigma_i\}_{i \in [k]} \subseteq \mathbb{F}_r$ such that

$$\sum_i \sigma_i \zeta_i = 0 \quad \text{and} \quad \sum_i \sigma_i \neq 0.$$

Our argument proceeds in two steps. In Section 3.2 we show that a k-nice sequence over $\mathbb{F}_r$ yields an infinite sequence of primes $\{p_i\}_{i \geq 1}$, where every $C_r^{p_i}$ contains a nontrivial k-dependence. In Sections 3.3 and 3.4, we show that C_r^p contains a nontrivial short dependence only if p is a large factor of a number $r^t - 1$.

3.2 A nice sequence yields short dependences between p-th roots

Our argument in this section has three steps. In Subsection 3.2.1, we study algebraically nice subsets of $\mathbb{F}_q^*$. In Subsection 3.2.2, we study combinatorially nice subsets of $\mathbb{F}_q^*$. Finally, in Subsection 3.2.3, we show how an interplay between the structural properties of algebraically and combinatorially nice subsets translates nice sequences over $\mathbb{F}_r$ into infinite families of primes p with short nontrivial dependences in C_r^p.

3.2.1 Algebraically nice subsets of $\mathbb{F}_q^*$

We start with a review of the definition of algebraic niceness (Definition 7). A subset $S \subseteq \mathbb{F}_q^*$ is called k-algebraically nice over $\mathbb{F}_r$ if there exist maps S_0, S_1 from $\mathbb{F}_q$ to $\mathbb{F}_r$ such that $\mathrm{supp}(S_0) \neq 0$, $\mathrm{supp}(S_1) \leq k$, $\sum_{\lambda \in \mathbb{F}_q} S_1(\lambda) \neq 0$, and for all $\alpha \in \mathbb{F}_q$, $\beta \in S$,

$$\sum_{\lambda \in \mathbb{F}_q} S_0(\alpha + \beta\lambda) S_1(\lambda) \neq 0.$$

The last constraint can be formulated equivalently as follows: for all $\alpha \in \mathbb{F}_q$ and $\beta \in S$,

$$\sum_{\lambda \in \mathbb{F}_q} S_0(\lambda) S_1((\lambda - \alpha)\beta^{-1}) \neq 0. \tag{3.3}$$

To proceed, we need some notation. Consider a finite field $\mathbb{F}_q = \mathbb{F}_{p^l}$, where p is prime. Fix a basis $e_1, \ldots, e_l$ of $\mathbb{F}_q$ over $\mathbb{F}_p$. In what follows, we shall often write $(\alpha_1, \ldots, \alpha_l) \in \mathbb{F}_p^l$ to denote

$$\alpha = \sum_{i=1}^{l} \alpha_i e_i \in \mathbb{F}_q.$$

Let r be a prime. Let R denote the ring

$$\mathbb{F}_r[x_1, \ldots, x_l]/(x_1^p - 1, \ldots, x_l^p - 1).$$

For $\alpha = (\alpha_1, \ldots, \alpha_l) \in \mathbb{F}_q$ we write x^α to denote the monomial $x_1^{\alpha_1} \ldots x_l^{\alpha_l} \in R$. Consider a natural one-to-one correspondence between maps $S_1 : \mathbb{F}_q \to \mathbb{F}_r$ and polynomials $\phi_{S_1}(x_1, \ldots, x_l) \in R$,

$$\phi_{S_1}(x_1, \ldots, x_l) = \sum_{\lambda \in \mathbb{F}_q} S_1(\lambda) x^\lambda.$$

It is easy to see that for all maps $S_1 : \mathbb{F}_q \to \mathbb{F}_r$ and for all fixed $\alpha \in \mathbb{F}_q$, $\beta \in \mathbb{F}_q^*$,

$$\phi_{S_1((\lambda-\alpha)\beta^{-1})}(x_1, \ldots, x_l) = \sum_{\lambda \in \mathbb{F}_q} S_1((\lambda - \alpha)\beta^{-1}) x^\lambda \tag{3.4}$$

$$= \sum_{\lambda \in \mathbb{F}_q} S_1(\lambda) x^{\alpha + \beta\lambda} = x_1^{\alpha_1} \ldots x_l^{\alpha_l} \phi_{S_1(\lambda/\beta)}(x_1, \ldots, x_l).$$

Let Γ be a family of maps $\mathbb{F}_q \to \mathbb{F}_r$. It is straightforward to verify that a map $S_0 : \mathbb{F}_q \to \mathbb{F}_r$ satisfies

$$\sum_{\lambda \in \mathbb{F}_q} S_0(\lambda) S_1(\lambda) = 0$$

for every $S_1 \in \Gamma$ if and only if ϕ_{S_0} belongs to $L^\perp$, where L is the linear subspace of R spanned by $\{\phi_{S_1}\}_{S_1 \in \Gamma}$.

Combining the last observation with (3.3) and (3.4), we conclude that a set $S \subseteq \mathbb{F}_q^*$ is k-algebraically nice over $\mathbb{F}_r$ if and only if there exists a map $S_1 : \mathbb{F}_q \to \mathbb{F}_r$ such that $\mathrm{supp}(S_1) \leq k$, $\sum_{\lambda \in \mathbb{F}_q} S_1(\lambda) \neq 0$, and the ideal generated by the polynomials

$$\left\{\phi_{S_1(\lambda/\beta)}\right\}_{\{\beta \in S\}}$$

is a *proper* ideal of R.

Note that polynomials $\{f_1, \ldots, f_h\}$ generate a proper ideal in R if and only if the polynomials

$$\{f_1, \ldots, f_h, x_1^p - 1, \ldots, x_l^p - 1\}$$

generate a proper ideal in $\mathbb{F}_r[x_1, \ldots, x_l]$. Note also that a family of polynomials generates a proper ideal in $\mathbb{F}_r[x_1, \ldots, x_l]$ if and only if it generates a proper ideal in $\overline{\mathbb{F}}_r[x_1, \ldots, x_l]$. Now, an application of Hilbert's *Nullstellensatz* [29, p. 168] implies that a set $S \subseteq \mathbb{F}_q^*$ is k-algebraically nice over $\mathbb{F}_r$ if and only if there exists a map $S_1 : \mathbb{F}_q \to \mathbb{F}_r$, with $\mathrm{supp}(S_1) \leq k$ and $\sum_{\lambda \in \mathbb{F}_q} S_1(\lambda) \neq 0$, such that the polynomials

$$\left\{\phi_{S_1(\lambda/\beta)}\right\}_{\{\beta \in S\}} \quad \text{and} \quad \left\{x_i^p - 1\right\}_{1 \leq i \leq l}$$

have a common root in $\overline{\mathbb{F}}_r$.

Lemma 18. *Let* $\mathbb{F}_q = \mathbb{F}_{p^l}$, *where* p *is prime. Suppose that* $\mathbb{F}_q$ *contains a subset that is nonempty and k-algebraically nice over* $\mathbb{F}_r$; *then there exists a nontrivial k-dependence in* C_r^p.

Proof. Assume that $S \subseteq \mathbb{F}_q^*$ is nonempty and k-algebraically nice over $\mathbb{F}_r$. The discussion above implies that there exists a map $S_1 : \mathbb{F}_q \to \mathbb{F}_r$ such that $\mathrm{supp}(S_1) \leq k$, $\sum_{\lambda \in \mathbb{F}_q} S_1(\lambda) \neq 0$, and all polynomials $\left\{\phi_{S_1(\lambda/\beta)}\right\}_{\{\beta \in S\}}$ vanish at some

$$(\zeta_1, \ldots, \zeta_l) \in (C_r^p)^l.$$

Fix an arbitrary $\beta_0 \in S$, and note that C_r^p is closed under multiplication. Thus,

$$\phi_{S_1(\lambda/\beta_0)}(\zeta_1, \ldots, \zeta_l) = 0 \tag{3.5}$$

yields a nontrivial k-dependence in C_r^p. $\qquad\square$

Note that Lemma 18 does not suffice to prove that a k-nice sequence $\left\{S_i \subseteq \mathbb{F}_{q_i}^*\right\}_{i \geq 1}$ over $\mathbb{F}_r$ yields infinitely many primes p with short nontrivial k-dependences in C_r^p. We need to argue that the set $\left\{\mathrm{char}\,\mathbb{F}_{q_i}\right\}_{i \geq 1}$ can not be finite.

To proceed, we need some more notation. Recall that $q = p^l$ and p is prime. For $x \in \mathbb{F}_q$, let

$$\mathrm{Tr}(x) = x + \ldots + x^{p^{l-1}} \in \mathbb{F}_p$$

denote the trace of x. For $\gamma \in \mathbb{F}_q, c \in \mathbb{F}_p^*$ we call the set

$$\pi_{\gamma,c} = \left\{x \in \mathbb{F}_q \mid \mathrm{Tr}(\gamma x) = c\right\}$$

a *proper-affine hyperplane* of $\mathbb{F}_q$.

Lemma 19. *Let* $\mathbb{F}_q = \mathbb{F}_{p^l}$, *where* p *is prime. Suppose that* $S \subseteq \mathbb{F}_q^*$ *is* k-*algebraically nice over* $\mathbb{F}_r$; *then there exist* $h \leq p^k$ *proper-affine hyperplanes* $\{\pi_{\gamma_r,c_r}\}_{1 \leq r \leq h}$ *of* $\mathbb{F}_q$ *such that*

$$S \subseteq \bigcup_{r=1}^{h} \pi_{\gamma_r,c_r}.$$

Proof. The discussion preceding Lemma 18 implies that there exists a map $S_1 : \mathbb{F}_q \rightarrow \mathbb{F}_r$ with $\mathrm{supp}(S_1) \leq k$ and $\sum_{\lambda \in \mathbb{F}_q} S_1(\lambda) \neq 0$ such that all polynomials $\{\phi_{S_1(\lambda/\beta)}\}_{\{\beta \in S\}}$ vanish at some

$$(\zeta_1, \ldots, \zeta_l) \in (C_r^p)^l.$$

Let ζ be a generator of C_p. For every $1 \leq i \leq l$, pick $\omega_i \in \mathbb{Z}_p$ such that $\zeta_i = \zeta^{\omega_i}$. Let

$$T = \{\tau \in \mathbb{F}_q \mid S_1(\tau) \neq 0\}.$$

Put $T = \{\tau_1, \ldots, \tau_{k'}\}$. Clearly, $k' \leq k$. For every $\beta \in S$,

$$\phi_{S_1(\lambda/\beta)}(\zeta_1, \ldots, \zeta_l) = 0$$

yields

$$\sum_{\lambda=(\lambda_1,\ldots,\lambda_l)\in\beta T} S_1(\lambda/\beta)\zeta^{\sum_{i=1}^{l}\lambda_i\omega_i} = 0. \tag{3.6}$$

Observe that for fixed values $\{\omega_i\}_{1 \leq i \leq l} \in \mathbb{Z}_p$, the map $D(\lambda) = \sum_{i=1}^{l} \lambda_i \omega_i$ is a linear map from $\mathbb{F}_q$ to $\mathbb{F}_p$. It is not hard to prove that every such map can be expressed as

$$D(\lambda) = \mathrm{Tr}(\delta\lambda)$$

for an appropriate choice of $\delta \in \mathbb{F}_q$. Therefore we can rewrite (3.6) as

$$\sum_{\lambda\in\beta T} S_1(\lambda/\beta)\zeta^{\mathrm{Tr}(\delta\lambda)} = \sum_{\tau\in T} S_1(\tau)\zeta^{\mathrm{Tr}(\delta\beta\tau)} = 0. \tag{3.7}$$

Let

$$W = \left\{(w_1, \ldots, w_{k'}) \in \mathbb{Z}_p^{k'} \mid S_1(\tau_1)\zeta^{w_1} + \ldots + S_1(\tau_{k'})\zeta^{w_{k'}} = 0\right\}$$

denote the set of exponents of the k'-dependences between powers of ζ. Clearly, $|W| \leq p^k$. The identity (3.7) implies that every $\beta \in S$ satisfies

$$\begin{cases} \mathrm{Tr}((\delta\tau_1)\beta) = w_1, \\ \;\;\vdots \\ \mathrm{Tr}((\delta\tau_{k'})\beta) = w_{k'}, \end{cases} \tag{3.8}$$

for an appropriate choice of $(w_1, \ldots, w_{k'}) \in W$. Note that the all-zeros vector does not lie in W, since

$$\sum_{\tau \in T} S_1(\tau) = \sum_{\lambda \in \mathbb{F}_q} S_1(\lambda) \neq 0.$$

Therefore at least one of the identities in (3.8) has a nonzero right-hand side, and defines a proper-affine hyperplane of $\mathbb{F}_q$. By collecting one such hyperplane for every element of W, we get a family of $|W|$ proper-affine hyperplanes containing every element of S. $\qquad\square$

3.2.2 Combinatorially nice subsets of $\mathbb{F}_q^*$

Lemma 19 gives us some insight into the structure of algebraically nice subsets of $\mathbb{F}_q$. Our next goal is to develop an insight into the structure of combinatorially nice subsets. We start by reviewing some relations between tensor and dot products of vectors. For vectors $\mathbf{u} \in \mathbb{F}_q^m$ and $\mathbf{v} \in \mathbb{F}_q^n$, let $\mathbf{u} \otimes \mathbf{v} \in \mathbb{F}_q^{mn}$ denote the tensor product of $\mathbf{u}$ and $\mathbf{v}$. The coordinates of $\mathbf{u} \otimes \mathbf{v}$ are labeled by all possible elements of $[m] \times [n]$ and

$$(\mathbf{u} \otimes \mathbf{v})_{i,j} = \mathbf{u}_i \mathbf{v}_j.$$

Also, let $\mathbf{u}^{\otimes l}$ denote the l-th tensor power of $\mathbf{u}$, and $\mathbf{u} \circ \mathbf{v}$ denote the concatenation of $\mathbf{u}$ and $\mathbf{v}$. The following identity is standard. For any $\mathbf{u}, \mathbf{x} \in \mathbb{F}_q^m$ and $\mathbf{v}, \mathbf{y} \in \mathbb{F}_q^n$,

$$(\mathbf{u} \otimes \mathbf{v}, \mathbf{x} \otimes \mathbf{y}) = \sum_{i \in [m], j \in [n]} \mathbf{u}_i \mathbf{v}_j \mathbf{x}_i \mathbf{y}_j \qquad (3.9)$$

$$= \left(\sum_{i \in [m]} \mathbf{u}_i \mathbf{x}_i \right) \left(\sum_{j \in [n]} \mathbf{v}_j \mathbf{y}_j \right) = (\mathbf{u}, \mathbf{x})(\mathbf{v}, \mathbf{y}).$$

In what follows, we need a generalization of the identity (3.9). Let

$$f(x_1, \ldots, x_h) = \sum_i c_i x_1^{\alpha_1^i} \ldots x_h^{\alpha_h^i}$$

be a polynomial in $\mathbb{F}_q[x_1, \ldots, x_h]$. Given f, we define $\bar{f} \in \mathbb{F}_q[x_1, \ldots, x_h]$ by

$$\bar{f} = \sum_i x_1^{\alpha_1^i} \ldots x_h^{\alpha_h^i},$$

i.e., we simply set all nonzero coefficients of f to 1. For vectors $\mathbf{u}_1, \ldots, \mathbf{u}_h$ in $\mathbb{F}_q^m$, we define

$$f(\mathbf{u}_1, \ldots, \mathbf{u}_h) = \circ_i c_i \mathbf{u}_1^{\otimes \alpha_1^i} \otimes \ldots \otimes \mathbf{u}_h^{\otimes \alpha_h^i}. \qquad (3.10)$$

Note that to obtain $f(\mathbf{u}_1, \ldots, \mathbf{u}_h)$, we have replaced products in f by tensor products and addition by concatenation. Clearly, $f(\mathbf{u}_1, \ldots, \mathbf{u}_h)$ is a vector whose dimension may be larger than m.

Claim. For every $f \in \mathbb{F}_q[x_1, \ldots, x_h]$ and vectors $\mathbf{u}_1, \ldots, \mathbf{u}_h, \mathbf{v}_1, \ldots, \mathbf{v}_h \in \mathbb{F}_q^m$,

$$\left(f(\mathbf{u}_1,\ldots,\mathbf{u}_h),\bar{f}(\mathbf{v}_1,\ldots,\mathbf{v}_h)\right) = f((\mathbf{u}_1,\mathbf{v}_1),\ldots,(\mathbf{u}_h,\mathbf{v}_h)). \qquad (3.11)$$

Proof. Let $\mathbf{u} = (\mathbf{u}_1,\ldots,\mathbf{u}_h)$ and $\mathbf{v} = (\mathbf{v}_1,\ldots,\mathbf{v}_h)$. Observe that if (3.11) holds for polynomials f_1 and f_2 defined over disjoint sets of monomials, then it also holds for $f = f_1 + f_2$:

$$\begin{aligned}
\left(f(\mathbf{u}),\bar{f}(\mathbf{v})\right) &= \left((f_1+f_2)(\mathbf{u}),(\bar{f}_1+\bar{f}_2)(\mathbf{v})\right)\\
&= \left(f_1(\mathbf{u}) \circ f_2(\mathbf{u}),\bar{f}_1(\mathbf{v}) \circ \bar{f}_2(\mathbf{v})\right)\\
&= f_1\left((\mathbf{u}_1,\mathbf{v}_1),\ldots,(\mathbf{u}_h,\mathbf{v}_h)\right) + f_2\left((\mathbf{u}_1,\mathbf{v}_1),\ldots,(\mathbf{u}_h,\mathbf{v}_h)\right)\\
&= f\left((\mathbf{u}_1,\mathbf{v}_1),\ldots,(\mathbf{u}_h,\mathbf{v}_h)\right).
\end{aligned}$$

Therefore it suffices to prove (3.11) for monomials $f = cx_1^{\alpha_1}\ldots x_h^{\alpha_h}$. It remains to note that the identity (3.11) for monomials $f = cx_1^{\alpha_1}\ldots x_h^{\alpha_h}$ follows immediately from (3.9) using induction on $\sum_{i=1}^{h}\alpha_i$. $\qquad\square$

The following lemma bounds combinatorial niceness of certain subsets of $\mathbb{F}_q^*$.

Lemma 20. *Let $\mathbb{F}_q = \mathbb{F}_{p^l}$, where p is prime. Let $S \subseteq \mathbb{F}_q^*$. Suppose there exist h proper-affine hyperplanes $\left\{\pi_{\gamma_r,c_r}\right\}_{1 \le r \le h}$ of $\mathbb{F}_q$ such that*

$$S \subseteq \bigcup_{r=1}^{h} \pi_{\gamma_r,c_r};$$

then S is at most $h(p-1)$-combinatorially nice.

Proof. Assume that S is t-combinatorially nice. This implies that for some $c > 0$ and every m, there exist two $n = \lfloor cm^t \rfloor$-sized collections of vectors $\{\mathbf{u}_i\}_{i\in[n]}$ and $\{\mathbf{v}_i\}_{i\in[n]}$ in $\mathbb{F}_q^m$, such that:

- For all $i \in [n]$, $(\mathbf{u}_i,\mathbf{v}_i) = 0$.
- For all $i,j \in [n]$ such that $i \ne j$, $(\mathbf{u}_j,\mathbf{v}_i) \in S$.

For a vector $\mathbf{u} \in \mathbb{F}_q^m$ and an integer e, let $\mathbf{u}^e$ denote the vector resulting from raising every coordinate of $\mathbf{u}$ to the power e. For every $i \in [n]$ and $r \in [h]$, define vectors $\mathbf{u}_i^{(r)}$ and $\mathbf{v}_i^{(r)}$ in $\mathbb{F}_q^{ml}$ by

$$\mathbf{u}_i^{(r)} = (\gamma_r \mathbf{u}_i) \circ (\gamma_r \mathbf{u}_i)^p \circ \ldots \circ (\gamma_r \mathbf{u}_i)^{p^{l-1}} \quad \text{and} \quad \mathbf{v}_i^{(r)} = \mathbf{v}_i \circ \mathbf{v}_i^p \circ \ldots \circ \mathbf{v}_i^{p^{l-1}}. \qquad (3.12)$$

Note that for every $r_1,r_2 \in [h]$, $\mathbf{v}_i^{(r_1)} = \mathbf{v}_i^{(r_2)}$. It is straightforward to verify that for every $i,j \in [n]$ and $r \in [h]$,

$$\left(\mathbf{u}_j^{(r)},\mathbf{v}_i^{(r)}\right) = \mathrm{Tr}(\gamma_r(\mathbf{u}_j,\mathbf{v}_i)). \qquad (3.13)$$

Combining (3.13) with the fact that S is covered by proper-affine hyperplanes $\left\{\pi_{\gamma_r,c_r}\right\}_{r\in[h]}$, we conclude that:

- For all $i \in [n]$ and $r \in [h]$. $\left(\mathbf{u}_i^{(r)}, \mathbf{v}_i^{(r)} \right) = 0$;

- For all $i, j \in [n]$ such that $i \neq j$, there exists $r \in [h]$ such that $\left(\mathbf{u}_j^{(r)}, \mathbf{v}_i^{(r)} \right) \in \mathbb{F}_p^*$.

Choose $g(x_1, \ldots, x_h) \in \mathbb{F}_p[x_1, \ldots, x_h]$ to be a homogeneous degree-h polynomial such that for $\mathbf{a} = (a_1, \ldots, a_h) \in \mathbb{F}_p^h$, $g(\mathbf{a}) = 0$ if and only if $\mathbf{a}$ is the all-zeros vector. The existence of such a (*norm*) polynomial g follows from [62, Example 6.7]. Set $f = g^{p-1}$. Note that for $\mathbf{a} \in \mathbb{F}_p^h$, $f(a) = 0$ if $\mathbf{a}$ is the all-zeros vector, and $f(\mathbf{a}) = 1$ otherwise. For all $i \in [n]$, define

$$\mathbf{u}_i' = f\left(\mathbf{u}_i^{(1)}, \ldots, \mathbf{u}_i^{(h)} \right) \circ (1) \quad \text{and} \quad \mathbf{v}_i' = \bar{f}\left(\mathbf{v}_i^{(1)}, \ldots, \mathbf{v}_i^{(h)} \right) \circ (-1). \quad (3.14)$$

Note that f and $\bar{f}$ are homogeneous degree-$(p-1)h$ polynomials in h variables. Therefore (3.10) implies that for all i, vectors $\mathbf{u}_i'$ and $\mathbf{v}_i'$ have dimension

$$m' \leq h^{(p-1)h} (ml)^{(p-1)h} + 1.$$

Combining the identities (3.14) and (3.11) and using the properties of dot products between vectors $\left\{ \mathbf{u}_i^{(r)} \right\}$ and $\left\{ \mathbf{v}_i^{(r)} \right\}$ discussed above, we conclude that for every m there exist two $n = \lfloor cm^t \rfloor$-sized collections of vectors $\{\mathbf{u}_i'\}_{i \in [n]}$ and $\{\mathbf{v}_i'\}_{i \in [n]}$ in $\mathbb{F}_q^{m'}$, such that:

- For all $i \in [n]$, $(\mathbf{u}_i', \mathbf{v}_i') = -1$.
- For all $i, j \in [n]$ such that $i \neq j$, $(\mathbf{u}_j, \mathbf{v}_i) = 0$.

Note that a family of vectors with such properties exists only if $n \leq m'$, i.e.,

$$\lfloor cm^t \rfloor \leq h^{(p-1)h} (ml)^{(p-1)h} + 1.$$

Given that we can pick m to be arbitrarily large, this implies that $t \leq (p-1)h$. $\quad \Box$

3.2.3 Summary

The next lemma presents the main result of this section.

Lemma 21. *Let r be a prime. Suppose there exists a k-nice sequence over $\mathbb{F}_r$; then for infinitely many primes p, there exists a nontrivial k-dependence in C_r^p.*

Proof. Assume that

$$\left\{ S_i \subseteq \mathbb{F}_{q_i}^* \right\}_{i \geq 1}$$

is a k-nice sequence over $\mathbb{F}_r$. Let p be a fixed prime. Combining Lemmas 19 and 20, we conclude that every subset $S \subseteq \mathbb{F}_{p^l}^*$ that is k-algebraically nice over $\mathbb{F}_r$ is at most $(p-1)p^k$-combinatorially nice. Note that our bound on the combinatorial niceness is independent of l. Therefore there are only finitely many extensions of the field $\mathbb{F}_p$ in the sequence $\{\mathbb{F}_{q_i}\}_{i \geq 1}$, and the set

$$\mathbb{P} = \{\operatorname{char} \mathbb{F}_{q_i}\}_{i \geq 1}$$

is infinite. It remains to note that, according to Lemma 18, for every $p \in \mathbb{P}$ there exists a nontrivial k-dependence in C_r^p. □

In what follows, we present necessary conditions for the existence of nontrivial k-dependences in C_r^p. We treat the $k = 3$ case separately, since in that case we can use a specialized argument to derive a slightly stronger conclusion.

3.3 k-dependences between p-th roots: a necessary condition

Lemma 22. *Let p and r be primes. Suppose there exists a nontrivial k-dependence in C_r^p; then*

$$\operatorname{ord}_p(r) \leq 2p^{1-1/(k-1)}. \tag{3.15}$$

Proof. Let $\{\zeta_i\}_{i \in [k]} \subseteq C_r^p$ and $\{\sigma_i\}_{i \in [k]} \subseteq \mathbb{F}_r$ be such that

$$\sum_{i \in [k]} \sigma_i \zeta_i = 0 \quad \text{and} \quad \sum_{i \in [k]} \sigma_i \neq 0.$$

Let $t = \operatorname{ord}_p(r)$. Note that $C_r^p \subseteq \mathbb{F}_{r^t}$. Note also that all elements of C_r^p other than the multiplicative identity are *proper* elements of $\mathbb{F}_{r^t}$ (i.e., they do not fall into a *proper* subfield of $\mathbb{F}_{r^t}$). Therefore, for every $\zeta \in C_r^p$ where $\zeta \neq 1$ and every nonzero $f(x) \in \mathbb{F}_r[x]$ such that $\deg f \leq t - 1$, we have $f(\zeta) \neq 0$.

By multiplying $\sum_{i=1}^k \sigma_i \zeta_i = 0$ through by ζ_k^{-1}, we may reduce the problem to the case $\zeta_k = 1$. Let ζ be the generator of C_r^p. For every $i \in [k-1]$, pick $w_i \in \mathbb{Z}_p$ such that $\zeta_i = \zeta^{w_i}$. We now have

$$\sum_{i=1}^{k-1} \sigma_i \zeta^{w_i} + \sigma_k = 0.$$

Set $h = \lfloor (t-1)/2 \rfloor$. For $m \in \mathbb{Z}_p$ and $i_1, \ldots, i_{k-1} \in [0, h]$, consider the following $(k-1)$-tuples:

$$(mw_1 + i_1, \ldots, mw_{k-1} + i_{k-1}) \in \mathbb{Z}_p^{k-1}. \tag{3.16}$$

Suppose that two of these coincide, say

$$(mw_1 + i_1, \ldots, mw_{k-1} + i_{k-1}) = (m'w_1 + i_1', \ldots, m'w_{k-1} + i_{k-1}'),$$

with $(m, i_1, \ldots, i_{k-1}) \neq (m', i_1', \ldots, i_{k-1}')$. Set $n = m - m'$ and $j_l = i_l' - i_l$ for $l \in [k-1]$. We now have

$$(nw_1, \ldots, nw_{k-1}) = (j_1, \ldots, j_{k-1})$$

with $-h \le j_1, \ldots, j_{k-1} \le h$. Observe that $n \neq 0$, and thus it has a multiplicative inverse $g \in \mathbb{Z}_p$. Consider the polynomial

$$P(z) = \sigma_1 z^{j_1+h} + \ldots + \sigma_{k-1} z^{j_{k-1}+h} + \sigma_k z^h \in \mathbb{F}_r[z].$$

Note that $\deg P \le 2h \le t - 1$. Note also that $P(1) \neq 0$ and $P(\zeta^g) = 0$. The latter identity contradicts the fact that ζ^g is a proper element of $\mathbb{F}_{r^t}$. This contradiction implies that all $(k-1)$-tuples in (3.16) are distinct. This yields

$$p^{k-1} \ge p\left(\frac{t}{2}\right)^{k-1},$$

which is equivalent to (3.15). □

3.4 3-dependences between p-th roots: a necessary condition

In this section we slightly strengthen Lemma 22 in the special case when $k = 3$. Our argument is loosely inspired by the Agrawal–Kayal–Saxena deterministic primality test [5].

Lemma 23. *Let p and r be primes. Suppose there exists a nontrivial three-dependence in C_r^p; then*

$$\operatorname{ord}_p(2) \le ((4/3)p)^{1/2}. \tag{3.17}$$

Proof. Let $\{\zeta_i\}_{i \in [3]} \subseteq C_r^p$ and $\{\sigma_i\}_{i \in [3]} \subseteq \mathbb{F}_r$ be such that

$$\sum_{i \in [3]} \sigma_i \zeta_i = 0 \quad \text{and} \quad \sum_{i \in [3]} \sigma_i \neq 0.$$

Let $t = \operatorname{ord}_p(r)$. Note that $C_r^p \subseteq \mathbb{F}_{r^t}$. Note also that all elements of C_r^p other than the multiplicative identity are proper elements of $\mathbb{F}_{r^t}$. Therefore, for every $\zeta \in C_r^p$ where $\zeta \neq 1$ and every nonzero $f(x) \in \mathbb{F}_r[x]$ such that $\deg f \le t - 1$, we have $f(\zeta) \neq 0$.

Without loss of generality, assume $\sigma_1 \neq 0, \sigma_3 = -1$, and $\zeta_3 = 1$. Observe that

$$\sigma_1 \zeta_1 + \sigma_2 \zeta_2 = 1$$

implies

$$\left(\sigma_1 \zeta_1 \zeta_2^{-1} + \sigma_2\right)^p = 1.$$

Put $\zeta = \zeta_1 \zeta_2^{-1}$. Note that $\zeta \neq 1$ (since $\sum_{i \in [3]} \sigma_i \neq 0$) and $\zeta, \sigma_1 \zeta + \sigma_2 \in C_r^p$. Consider the products

$$\pi_{i,j} = \zeta^i (\sigma_1 \zeta + \sigma_2)^j \in C_r^p \quad \text{for } 0 \le i, j \le t - 1.$$

Note that $\pi_{i,j}, \pi_{k,l}$ cannot be the same if $i \ge k$ and $l \ge j$, as then

$$\zeta^{i-k} - (\sigma_1 \zeta + \sigma_2)^{l-j} = 0,$$

but the left-hand side has degree less than t. In other words, if $\pi_{i,j} = \pi_{k,l}$ and $(i,j) \neq (k,l)$, then the pairs (i,j) and (k,l) are comparable under termwise comparison. In particular, either $(k,l) = (i+a, j+b)$ or $(i,j) = (k+a, l+b)$ for some pair (a,b) with $\pi_{a,b} = 1$.

We next check that there cannot be two distinct nonzero pairs $(a,b), (a',b')$ with

$$\pi_{a,b} = \pi_{a',b'} = 1.$$

As above, these pairs must be comparable; we may assume without loss of generality that $a \leq a', b \leq b'$. The equations $\pi_{a,b} = 1$ and $\pi_{a'-a,b'-b} = 1$ force $a+b \geq t$ and $(a'-a) + (b'-b) \geq t$, so $a'+b' \geq 2t$. But $a',b' \leq t-1$, and hence there is a contradiction.

If there is no nonzero pair (a,b) with $0 \leq a,b \leq t-1$ and $\pi_{a,b} = 1$, then all $\pi_{i,j}$ are distinct, so $p \geq t^2$. Otherwise, as above, the pair (a,b) is unique, and the pairs (i,j) with $0 \leq i,j \leq t-1$ and $(i,j) \not\geq (a,b)$ are pairwise distinct. The number of pairs excluded by the condition $(i,j) \not\geq (a,b)$ is $(t-a)(t-b)$; since $a+b \geq t$, $(t-a)(t-b) \leq t^2/4$. Hence $p \geq t^2 - t^2/4 = 3t^2/4$ as desired.   □

3.5 Summary

In Section 3.1, we argued that in order to use the point removal method to obtain k-query locally decodable codes of length $\exp(n^\varepsilon)$ over $\mathbb{F}_r$ for some fixed k and all $\varepsilon > 0$, one needs to exhibit a sequence of subsets of finite fields that is k-nice over $\mathbb{F}_r$. In what follows, we use the technical results of the previous sections to show that the existence of a k-nice sequence over $\mathbb{F}_r$ implies that infinitely many Mersenne-type numbers $r^t - 1$ have large prime factors.

Theorem 10. *Let r be a prime. Suppose there exists a sequence of subsets of finite fields that is k-nice over $\mathbb{F}_r$; then, for infinitely many values of t, we have*

$$P(r^t - 1) \geq \left(\frac{t}{2}\right)^{1+1/(k-2)}. \tag{3.18}$$

Proof. Using Lemmas 21 and 22, we conclude that a k-nice sequence yields infinitely many primes p such that $\text{ord}_p(r) \leq 2p^{1-1/(k-1)}$. Let p be such a prime and $t = \text{ord}_p(r)$. Then $P(r^t - 1) \geq (t/2)^{1+1/(k-2)}$.   □

A combination of Lemmas 21 and 23 yields a slightly stronger bound for the special case of 3-nice sequences.

Theorem 11. *Let r be a prime. Suppose there exists a sequence of subsets of finite fields that is three-nice over $\mathbb{F}_r$; then, for infinitely many values of t, we have*

$$P(r^t - 1) \geq \left(\frac{3}{4}\right) t^2. \tag{3.19}$$

We would like to remind the reader that although (in the case $r = 2$) the lower bounds for $P(r^t - 1)$ given by (3.18) and (3.19) are extremely weak in light of the widely accepted conjecture that the number of Mersenne primes is infinite, they are substantially stronger than what is currently known unconditionally (3.1).

3.6 Conclusions

Our results in this chapter show that any attempts to obtain locally decodable codes of length $\exp(n^\varepsilon)$ for some fixed query complexity and all $\varepsilon > 0$ via the point removal method (i.e., via Proposition 4) require progress on an old number theory problem. Therefore obtaining such codes using this technique seems unlikely in the near future.

Our result should be used to direct the efforts of researchers looking for better constructions of locally decodable codes. Specifically, the author hopes [96, section 7] that although point removal in finite fields has reached a solid barrier, there still may be room for further progress via generalizations of the point removal idea to suitably chosen finite commutative rings.

3.7 Addendum

The barrier to better constructions of locally decodable codes via the point removal method established in this chapter did not stand long. In 2008, Efremenko [38] found a way to circumvent it by generalizing the code construction to work over rings of integers modulo composites rather than over finite fields.

Specifically, Efremenko replaced the field $\mathbb{F}_q$ by a ring $\mathbb{Z}_b$ for a composite b in Definitions 6, 5, and 7, and used a powerful result of Grolmusz [49] showing that certain subsets of $\mathbb{Z}_b$ are combinatorially far "nicer" than any subsets of $\mathbb{F}_q$ to obtain substantial improvements in upper bounds for the codeword length. In particular, Efremenko [38] obtained the first families of three-query LDCs that unconditionally have subexponential length. Efremenko's results have been extended in [20, 36, 55].

Chapter 4
Private information retrieval

In this chapter we turn our attention to the second main subject of the book, namely, private information retrieval. Recall that private information retrieval schemes are cryptographic protocols designed to safeguard the privacy of database users by allowing clients to retrieve records from replicated databases while completely hiding the identity of the retrieved records from the database owners.

We address the main parameters of interest in private information retrieval schemes, namely the number of servers involved in the scheme and the communication complexity, which is the number of bits exchanged between a user accessing a database and the servers. We obtain new upper and lower bounds for the efficiency of such schemes.

In the first part of the chapter (Section 4.2), we deal with upper bounds. We use the point removal method described in Chapter 2 to obtain a new generation of PIR schemes. Our constructions yield large improvements in the communication complexity of schemes involving three or more servers.

Sections 4.3–4.5 constitute the second (lower-bounds) part of this chapter. In Section 4.3, we introduce a new restricted (bilinear group-based) model of two-server private information retrieval. Our model is fairly broad and captures all currently known two-server schemes. In Section 4.4, we obtain a tight lower bound for the communication complexity of bilinear group-based PIR schemes. Finally, in Section 4.5, we discuss possible interpretations of our lower bound.

4.1 Preliminaries

We model the database by an r-ary string of length n. A k-server PIR scheme involves k servers $\mathscr{S}_1, \ldots, \mathscr{S}_k$, each holding the same the database $\mathbf{x} \in [r]^n$, and a user $\mathscr{U}$ who knows n and wants to retrieve some value $\mathbf{x}_i$, $i \in [n]$, without revealing any information about the value of i to the servers. We restrict our attention to one-round information-theoretic PIR protocols. Below is a formal definition of a PIR scheme.

S. Yekhanin, *Locally Decodable Codes and Private Information Retrieval Schemes*,
Information Security and Cryptography, DOI 10.1007/978-3-642-14358-8_4,
© Springer-Verlag Berlin Heidelberg 2010

Definition 11. A k-server private information retrieval protocol is a triplet of non-uniform algorithms $\mathscr{P} = (\mathscr{Q}, \mathscr{A}, \mathscr{C})$. We assume that each algorithm has been given the value of n as an advice. At the beginning of the protocol, the user $\mathscr{U}$ tosses random coins and obtains a random string $\mathbf{s}$. Next $\mathscr{U}$ invokes $\mathscr{Q}(i, \mathbf{s})$ to generate a k-tuple of queries $(\text{que}_1, \ldots, \text{que}_k)$. For $j \in [k]$, $\mathscr{U}$ sends que_j to $\mathscr{S}_j$. Each server $\mathscr{S}_j$, $j \in [k]$ responds with an answer $\text{ans}_j = \mathscr{A}(j, \mathbf{x}, \text{que}_j)$. Finally, $\mathscr{U}$ computes his/her output by applying the reconstruction algorithm $\mathscr{C}(\text{ans}_1, \ldots, \text{ans}_k, i, \mathbf{s})$. The protocol must satisfy the following requirements:

- Correctness. For any n, $\mathbf{x} \in [r]^n$, and $i \in [n]$, $\mathscr{U}$ obtains the correct value of $\mathbf{x}_i$ with probability 1 (where the probability is over the random strings $\mathbf{s}$).
- Privacy. Each server individually learns no information about i. More precisely, we require that for any n and for any $j \in [k]$, the distributions $\text{que}_j(i, \mathbf{s})$ are identical for all values $i \in [n]$.

The *communication complexity* of a private information retrieval protocol $\mathscr{P}$ is a function of n measuring the total number of bits communicated between the user and the servers, maximized over all choices of $\mathbf{x} \in [r]^n$, $i \in [n]$, and random inputs.

In the special case where r is a prime power and the elements of the alphabet $[r]$ are in one-to-one correspondence with the elements of the finite field $\mathbb{F}_r$, it makes sense to talk about *linear* private information retrieval schemes [48]. A linear PIR scheme is a PIR scheme where the answer function $\mathscr{A}(j, \mathbf{x}, \text{que}_j)$ is linear in $\mathbf{x}$ over $\mathbb{F}_r$ for arbitrary fixed values of j and que_j. In other words, every coordinate of an answer is a linear combination of the database values.

4.2 From LDCs to PIR schemes

In this section, we present our improvements of the upper bounds for the communication complexity of private information retrieval.

Our improvements follow via a relatively simple reduction that turns the constructions of locally decodable codes presented in Chapter 2 into constructions of private information retrieval schemes. Note that there are known generic procedures [56] to convert LDCs into PIR schemes. However, a simple application of such a procedure to our LDCs would yield either a PIR protocol with perfect privacy but a small probability of error, or a PIR protocol with perfect correctness but some slight privacy leakage. Fortunately, it is possible to achieve both perfect privacy and perfect correctness simultaneously via a specially designed argument.

We now turn to Lemma 4, which is the core lemma of Chapter 2. That lemma translates nice subsets of finite fields to codes. We show how a minor modification to the proof of the lemma allows us to build private information retrieval schemes from nice sets. Before we proceed, we slightly strengthen the definition of combinatorially nice sets.

Definition 12. Let q be a prime power. A set $S \subseteq \mathbb{F}_q^*$ is called (m,n)-normally combinatorially nice if there exist two families of vectors $\{\mathbf{u}_1, \ldots, \mathbf{u}_n\}$, $\{\mathbf{v}_1, \ldots, \mathbf{v}_n\}$ and a vector $\mathbf{e}$ in $\mathbb{F}_q^m$ such that:

- For all $i \in [n]$, $(\mathbf{u}_i, \mathbf{v}_i) = 0$.
- For all $i, j \in [n]$ such that $i \neq j$, $(\mathbf{u}_j, \mathbf{v}_i) \in S$.
- For all $i \in [n]$, $(\mathbf{u}_i, \mathbf{e}) \neq 0$.

Clearly, every normally combinatorially nice set is combinatorially nice. The converse also holds for all the specific combinatorially nice sets that have been considered in this book. Our only construction of combinatorially nice sets is given by Lemma 6. It is straightforward to verify that the all-ones vector $\mathbf{e} \in \mathbb{F}_p^m$ is nonorthogonal to every vector $\mathbf{u}_i$ considered in that lemma. Our proof of Lemma 24 assumes the reader's familiarity with the proof of Lemma 4. We write $\log z$ to denote the logarithm to base 2.

Lemma 24. *Let q be a prime power and let r be a prime. Assume that $S \subseteq \mathbb{F}_q^*$ is simultaneously (m,n)-normally combinatorially nice, and k-algebraically nice over $\mathbb{F}_r$. The set S yields an $\mathbb{F}_r$-linear k-server PIR scheme with questions of bit length $m \log q$ and answers of bit length $q \log r$ that allows private retrieval of coordinate values from an r-ary database of length n.*

Proof. In the preprocessing stage, the servers encode the database $\mathbf{x}$ with a k-query locally decodable code C obtained from Lemma 4. We shall use the notation of that lemma. Recall that the coordinates of $C(\mathbf{x})$ are in one-to-one correspondence with points in $\mathbb{F}_q^m$. In order to decode $\mathbf{x}_i$, the user has to query $\mathrm{supp}(S_1)$ locations

$$\{\mathbf{w} + \lambda \mathbf{v}_i \mid \lambda : S_1(\lambda) \neq 0\}$$

for some $\mathbf{w} \in T_i$, where T_i is the union of certain cosets of the hyperplane

$$\{\mathbf{y} \in \mathbb{F}_q^m \mid (\mathbf{u}_i, \mathbf{y}) = 0\}.$$

Unlike the case of the LDC setup, in the PIR setup the user cannot pick $\mathbf{w} \in T_i$ uniformly at random and then query the locations

$$\{\mathbf{w} + \lambda \mathbf{v}_i \mid \lambda : S_1(\lambda) \neq 0\}$$

from $\mathrm{supp}(S_1)$ different servers, since in such a case the servers would observe a uniform distribution on T_i rather than a uniform distribution on $\mathbb{F}_q^m$. Here is our way around this problem.

Let $\mathbf{e} \in \mathbb{F}_q^m$ be such that $(\mathbf{u}_i, \mathbf{e}) \neq 0$ for all $i \in [n]$. Thus, for every $i \in [n]$ and every $\mathbf{w} \in \mathbb{F}_q^m$, there is some $\gamma_0 \in \mathbb{F}_q$ such that $\mathbf{w} + \gamma_0 \mathbf{e} \in T_i$. The user picks $\mathbf{w} \in \mathbb{F}_q^m$ uniformly at random and (simultaneously) asks q $\mathrm{supp}(S_1)$-tuples of queries of the form

$$\{\mathbf{w} + \gamma \mathbf{e} + \lambda \mathbf{v}_i \mid \lambda : S_1(\lambda) \neq 0\}$$

for all $\gamma \in \mathbb{F}_q$. For every $\mathrm{supp}(S_1)$-tuple and for every $j \in [\mathrm{supp}(S_1)]$, the query number j goes to the server $\mathscr{S}_j$. (Note that in order to ask all these queries, the user needs to communicate only a single point in $\mathbb{F}_q^m$ to each of the servers.) It is easy to verify that in such a case each server individually observes a uniform distribution independent of i, while the user always successfully reconstructs $\mathbf{x}_i$ from one of the supp(S_1)-tuples of queries. □

Recall that we have two definitions of combinatorial niceness, one involving two parameters (Definition 5) and the other involving a single parameter (Definition 6). Similarly, we would like to have two definitions of normal combinatorial niceness. Therefore we define a set $S \subseteq \mathbb{F}_q^*$ to be t-normally combinatorially nice if there exists a constant $c > 0$ such that for all positive integers m, S is $(m, \lfloor cm^t \rfloor)$-normally combinatorially nice.

Below is a variant of Lemma 24 involving a single-parameter definition of normal combinatorial niceness. The proof is essentially identical to the proof of Proposition 4 and is omitted.

Lemma 25. *Let q be a prime power and let r be a prime. Assume that $S \subseteq \mathbb{F}_q^*$ is simultaneously t-normally combinatorially nice, and k-algebraically nice over $\mathbb{F}_r$. For every database length n, the set S yields an $\mathbb{F}_r$-linear k-server private information retrieval scheme with questions of bit length $O\left(n^{1/t}\right)$ and answers of bit length $O(1)$.*

In what follows, we use our constructions of normally combinatorially nice and algebraically nice sets presented in Sections 2.5 and 2.6 together with Lemmas 24 and 25 to construct efficient private information retrieval schemes.

In Section 4.2.1, we present our results for the narrow case of three-server binary PIR schemes. Firstly, we show that given a single Mersenne prime $p = 2^t - 1$, one can design three-server binary PIR schemes with $O\left(n^{1/(t+1)}\right)$ communication to access an n-bit database, for every n. Secondly, we use some of the achievements of the centuries-old study of Mersenne primes, and present large explicit improvements upon earlier work.

In Section 4.2.2, we present the general form of our results. We show that if r is a prime and $r^t - 1$ has a polynomially large prime factor $p \geq r^{\gamma t}$, then for every database length n there exists a $k(\gamma)$-server r-ary PIR scheme with $O\left(n^{1/(t+1)}\right)$ communication. The number of servers in our such a scheme depends on the size of the largest prime factor of $r^t - 1$, and the communication complexity depends on the size of $r^t - 1$ itself. The larger the largest prime factor is, the smaller is the number of servers. The larger $r^t - 1$ is, the smaller is the communication complexity.

4.2.1 Upper bounds for three-server binary PIR schemes

Combining Lemma 25 with Lemmas 7 and 14, we conclude that every Mersenne prime $p = 2^t - 1$ yields a family of three-server private information retrieval schemes with $O\left(n^{1/t}\right)$ communication.

Theorem 12. *Let $p = 2^t - 1$ be a fixed Mersenne prime. For every database length n there exists a three-server binary PIR protocol with questions of length $O\left(n^{1/t}\right)$ and answers of length $O(1)$.*

A generic balancing technique [28, section 4.3] allows one to convert any private information retrieval protocol with questions of length $O\left(n^{1/t}\right)$ and answers of length $O(1)$ into a new PIR protocol with $O\left(n^{1/(t+1)}\right)$ total communication. Such a conversion yields the following theorem.

Theorem 13. *Let $p = 2^t - 1$ be a fixed Mersenne prime. For every database length n, there exists a three-server binary PIR protocol with $O\left(n^{1/(t+1)}\right)$ communication.*

Plugging the value of the largest known Mersenne prime $p = 2^{32\ 582\ 657} - 1$ into Theorem 13, we conclude the following.

Theorem 14. *For every database length n there exists a three-server binary PIR protocol with a communication complexity of $O\left(n^{1/32\ 582\ 658}\right)$.*

The next two theorems capture the asymptotic parameters of our private information retrieval schemes under some number-theoretic assumptions. Both theorems follow easily from a combination of Lemma 24 with Lemmas 7 and 14 using arguments that are essentially identical to the proofs of Theorems 4 and 5.

Theorem 15. *Suppose that the number of Mersenne primes is infinite; then for infinitely many database lengths n, there exists a three-server binary PIR protocol with a communication complexity of $n^{O(1/\log\log n)}$.*

Theorem 16. *Let ε be a positive constant. Suppose that Conjecture 1 (Section 2.7.1) regarding the density of Mersenne primes holds; then for every database length n, there exists a three-server binary PIR protocol with a communication complexity of $n^{O\left(1/\log^{1-\varepsilon}\log n\right)}$.*

4.2.2 Upper bounds for general PIR schemes

For an integer m, let $P(m)$ denote the largest prime factor of m. Our first theorem below gets three-server r-ary private information retrieval schemes from numbers $m = r^t - 1$ with prime factors larger than $m^{3/4}$. The proof is essentially identical to the proof of Theorem 6 and is obtained by combining Lemmas 7, 15, and 25.

Theorem 17. *Let r be a prime. Suppose that $P(r^t - 1) > r^{0.75t}$; then for every database length n, there exists a three-server r-ary PIR protocol with questions of length $O\left(n^{1/t}\right)$ and answers of length $O(1)$.*

Theorem 17 immediately yields the following.

Theorem 18. *Let r be a prime. Suppose, for infinitely many t, we have $P(r^t - 1) > r^{0.75t}$; then for every $\varepsilon > 0$, there exists a family of three-server r-ary PIR protocols with questions of length $O(n^\varepsilon)$ and answers of length $O(1)$.*

The next theorem gets PIR schemes involving a constant number of servers from numbers $m = r^t - 1$ with prime factors larger than m^γ for every value of γ. The proof is essentially identical to the proof of Theorem 8 and is obtained by combining Lemmas 7, 16, and 25.

Theorem 19. *Let r be a prime. For every $\gamma > 0$, there exists an integer $k = k(\gamma, r)$ such that the following implication holds. Suppose that $P(r^t - 1) > r^{\gamma t}$; then for every database length n, there exists a k-server r-ary PIR protocol with questions of length $O\left(n^{1/t}\right)$ and answers of length $O(1)$.*

We obtain the following as an immediate corollary.:

Theorem 20. *Let r be a prime. Suppose, for some $\gamma > 0$ and infinitely many t, we have $P(r^t - 1) > r^{\gamma t}$; then there is a fixed k such that for every $\varepsilon > 0$, there exists a family of k-server r-ary PIR protocols with questions of length $O\left(n^\varepsilon\right)$ and answers of length $O(1)$.*

4.3 A combinatorial view of two-server PIR

This section begins the second (lower-bounds) part of this chapter. We introduce a new combinatorial interpretation of two-server PIR, and identify the models of bilinear PIR and bilinear group-based PIR. We start with some definitions.

Definition 13. A generalized Latin square $Q = \text{GLS}[n, T]$ is a square matrix of size $T \times T$ over the alphabet $[n] \cup \{*\}$, such that:

* For every $i \in [n]$ and $j \in [T]$, there exists a unique $k \in [T]$ such that $Q_{jk} = i$.
* For every $i \in [n]$ and $j \in [T]$, there exists a unique $k \in [T]$ such that $Q_{kj} = i$.

In particular, every row (and every column) of $\text{GLS}[n, T]$ contains precisely $(T - n)$ stars. We call the ratio n/T the *density* of the generalized Latin square. It is easy to see that generalized Latin squares of density 1 are simply Latin squares.

Let $Q = \text{GLS}[n, T]$, and let $\sigma : [n] \to [r]$ be an arbitrary map. We denote by Q_σ a matrix of size $T \times T$ over the alphabet $[r] \cup \{*\}$, which is obtained from Q by replacing every nonstar entry i in Q by $\sigma(i)$. We say that a matrix $C \in [r]^{T \times T}$ is a *completion* of Q_σ if $C_{ij} = (Q_\sigma)_{ij}$ whenever $(Q_\sigma)_{ij} \in [r]$.

For matrices $C \in [r]^{c \times c}$ and $A \in [r]^{l \times l}$, we say that C *reduces* to A if there exist two maps $\pi_1 : [c] \to [l]$ and $\pi_2 : [c] \to [l]$ such that for any $j, k \in [c]$, $C_{jk} = A_{\pi_1(j), \pi_2(k)}$. Note that we do not impose any restrictions on the maps π_1 and π_2; in particular, c can be larger then l.

Definition 14. Let $Q = \text{GLS}[n, T]$, and $A \in [r]^{l \times l}$. We say that A *covers* Q, (notation $Q \hookrightarrow A$) if for every $\sigma : [n] \to [r]$, there exists a completion C of Q_σ such that C reduces to A.

Theorem 21. *The following two implications are valid:*

- *A pair $Q \hookrightarrow A$, where $Q = GLS[n, T]$ and $A \in [r]^{l \times l}$, yields a two-server r-ary private information retrieval protocol with communication $\log T$ from $\mathcal{U}$ to each server $\mathcal{S}_j$ and communication $\log l$ from the $\mathcal{S}_j$'s back to $\mathcal{U}$.*
- *A two-server r-ary PIR protocol with queries of length $t(n)$ and answers of length $a(n)$, where the user tosses at most $\tau(n)$ random coins, yields a pair $Q \hookrightarrow A$, where $Q = GLS\left[n, nr^{t(n)+\tau(n)}\right]$, and A is an r-ary square matrix of size $nr^{t(n)+a(n)}$.*

Proof. We start with the first part. We assume that the matrix A is known to all parties $\mathcal{U}, \mathcal{S}_1$, and $\mathcal{S}_2$. In the preprocessing stage, the servers use the database $\mathbf{x} \in [r]^n$ to define the map $\sigma : [n] \to [r]$, setting $\sigma(i) = \mathbf{x}_i$. Also, they find an appropriate completion C, and fix the maps $\pi_1 : [T] \to [l]$ and $\pi_2 : [T] \to [l]$ such for all j, k, $C_{jk} = A_{\pi_1(j), \pi_2(k)}$. Next, the following protocol is executed.

$\mathcal{U}$	: Picks a location j, k in Q such that $Q_{jk} = i$ uniformly at random.
$\mathcal{U} \to \mathcal{S}_1 : j$	
$\mathcal{U} \to \mathcal{S}_2 : k$	
$\mathcal{U} \leftarrow \mathcal{S}_1 : \pi_1(j)$	
$\mathcal{U} \leftarrow \mathcal{S}_2 : \pi_2(k)$	
$\mathcal{U}$	: Outputs $A_{\pi_1(j), \pi_2(k)}$.

It is straightforward to verify that the protocol above is private, since a uniformly random choice of a location j, k such that $Q_{jk} = i$ induces uniformly random individual distributions on j and on k. The correctness follows from the fact that C reduces to A. The total communication is given by $2(\log T + \log l)$.

Now we proceed to the second part. Consider a two-server protocol $\mathcal{P} = (\mathcal{Q}, \mathcal{A}, \mathcal{C})$. First we show that one can modify $\mathcal{P}$ to obtain a new private information retrieval protocol $\mathcal{P}' = (\mathcal{Q}', \mathcal{A}', \mathcal{C}')$ such that $\mathcal{C}'$ depends only on ans_1' and ans_2', and not on i or $\mathbf{s}$. The transformation is simple:

- First, $\mathcal{Q}'$ obtains a random string $\mathbf{s}$ and invokes $\mathcal{Q}(i, \mathbf{s})$ to generate the queries $(\text{que}_1, \text{que}_2)$. Next, $\mathcal{Q}'$ tosses $\log n$ extra random coins to represent i as a random sum $i = i_1 + i_2 \mod (n)$, sets $\text{que}_1' = \text{que}_1 \circ i_1$ and $\text{que}_2' = \text{que}_2 \circ i_2$, and sends que_1' to $\mathcal{S}_1$ and que_2' to $\mathcal{S}_2$.
- For $j = 1, 2$, the algorithm $\mathcal{A}'$ extracts que_j from que_j', runs $\mathcal{A}$ on $(j, \mathbf{x}, \text{que}_j)$, and returns $\text{ans}_j \circ \text{que}_j'$.
- Finally, $\mathcal{C}'$ extracts $\text{que}_1, \text{que}_2, \text{ans}_1, \text{ans}_2$, and i from ans_1' and ans_2' and performs a brute force search over all possible random coin tosses of $\mathcal{Q}$ to find some random input $\mathbf{s}'$ such that $\mathcal{Q}(i, \mathbf{s}') = (\text{que}_1, \text{que}_2)$. $\mathcal{C}'$ runs $\mathcal{C}$ on $(\text{ans}_1, \text{ans}_2, i, \mathbf{s}')$ and returns the answer. Note that the string $\mathbf{s}'$ may in fact be different from the string $\mathbf{s}$; however, the correctness property of $\mathcal{P}$ implies that $\mathcal{C}'$ outputs the right value even in this case.

Now consider the protocol $\mathcal{P}'$. Let Q_j' denote the range of queries to server j, and A_j' denote the range of answers from server j. The variable que_j' ranges over Q_j', and the variable ans'_j ranges over A'_j. Let $R(que'_j, i)$ denote the set of random strings $\mathbf{s}$ that lead to query que'_j to server j on input i. Formally,

$$R(que'_1, i) = \left\{ \mathbf{s} \in [r]^{\tau(n)} \mid \exists\, que'_2 : Q(i, \mathbf{s}) = (que'_1, que'_2) \right\},$$

$$R(que'_2, i) = \left\{ \mathbf{s} \in [r]^{\tau(n)} \mid \exists\, que'_1 : Q(i, \mathbf{s}) = (que'_1, que'_2) \right\}.$$

Note that the privacy property of the protocol $\mathscr{P}'$ implies that the cardinalities of $R(que'_j, i)$ are independent of i. We denote these cardinalities by $\mathbf{s}(que'_j)$. It is easy to see that $\mathbf{s}(que'_j)$ is always an integer between 1 and $r^{\tau(n)}$. Now we are ready to define the matrices Q and A.

The rows of Q are labeled by pairs (que'_1, s_1), where $s_1 \in [\mathbf{s}(que'_1)]$. The columns of Q are labeled by pairs (que'_2, s_2), where $s_2 \in [\mathbf{s}(que'_2)]$. We set $Q_{(que'_1, s_1), (que'_2, s_2)} = i$ if there exists a string $\mathbf{s} \in R(que'_1, i) \cap R(que'_2, i)$ such that $\mathbf{s}$ is the string number s_1 in $R(que'_1, i)$ and the string number s_2 in $R(que'_2, i)$ with respect to the lexicographic ordering of these sets; otherwise we set $Q_{(que'_1, s_1), (que'_2, s_2)} = *$.

Consider an arbitrary pair $(i, (que'_1, s_1))$, where $s_1 \in [\mathbf{s}(que'_1)]$. Let $\mathbf{s}$ be the random string number s_1 in the lexicographic ordering of $R(que'_1, i)$. Let $\mathcal{Q}'(i, \mathbf{s}) = (que'_1, que'_2)$, and let s_2 be the number of $\mathbf{s}$ in the lexicographic ordering of $R(que'_2, i)$. The column of Q labeled (que'_2, s_2) is the unique column such that

$$Q_{(que'_1, s_1), (que'_2, s_2)} = i.$$

Thus we have proved that every row of Q contains exactly one entry labeled i. A similar argument proves this claim for columns. Thus Q is a generalized Latin square.

Now we proceed to the matrix A. The rows of A are labeled by possible values of ans'_1, similarly, the columns of A are labeled by possible values of ans'_2. We set

$$A_{ans'_1, ans'_2} = \mathscr{C}'(ans'_1, ans'_2).$$

The unspecified entries of A are set arbitrarily. The matrix A defined above need not be a square; however, one can always pad it to a square shape.

It remains to show that $Q \hookrightarrow A$. Given a map $\sigma : [n] \to [r]$, we consider a database $\mathbf{x}$, where $\mathbf{x}_i = \sigma(i)$. We use the protocol $\mathscr{P}'$ to define maps π_1 from the row set of Q to the row set of A, and π_2 from the column set of Q to the column set of A. We set $\pi_1(que'_1, s_1) = \mathscr{A}'(1, \mathbf{x}, que'_1)$ and $\pi_2(que'_2, s_2) = \mathscr{A}'(2, \mathbf{x}, que'_2)$. The correctness property of $\mathscr{P}'$ implies that the maps π_1, π_2 reduce the certain completion of Q_σ to A. $\square$

The theorem above represents our combinatorial view of two-server PIR protocols. A PIR protocol is just a pair $Q \hookrightarrow A$, where Q is a generalized Latin square and A is an r-ary matrix. Every PIR protocol can be converted into this form, and in the case the number of the user's coin tosses is linear in the query length, such a conversion does not affect the asymptotic communication complexity.

4.3.1 Bilinear PIR

The combinatorial interpretation of private information retrieval suggested above views PIR as a problem of reducing certain special families of matrices to some fixed matrix. A nice example of a nontrivial matrix where one can say a lot about matrices that reduce to it is the Hadamard matrix. In what follows, we assume that the alphabet size r is a prime power.

Definition 15. A Hadamard matrix H_t is an $r^t \times r^t$ matrix whose rows and columns are labeled by elements of $\mathbb{F}_r^t$ and whose matrix cells contain the dot products of the corresponding labels, i.e., $(H_t)_{\mathbf{v}_1, \mathbf{v}_2} = (\mathbf{v}_1, \mathbf{v}_2)$.

Lemma 26. *Let M be a square matrix with entries from $\mathbb{F}_r$; then M reduces to the Hadamard matrix H_t if and only if the rank of M is at most t.*

Proof. Clearly, the rank of H_t is t, and therefore the rank of any matrix that reduces to H_t is at most that large. To prove the converse, observe that M can be written as a sum of t matrices

$$M = M^1 + \ldots + M^t,$$

where each M^j is of rank at most one. Let m be the size of M. For every $i \in [t]$, set the i-th coordinate of the vectors $\mathbf{v}^1, \ldots, \mathbf{v}^m$ $\mathbf{u}^1, \ldots, \mathbf{u}^m$ of length t so that

$$v_i^j u_i^k = M_{jk}^i.$$

Now the maps $\pi_1 : [m] \to [r^t]$, $\pi_2 : [m] \to [r^t]$ defined by $\pi_1(j) = \mathbf{v}^j$, $\pi_2(k) = \mathbf{u}^k$ reduce M to H_t.   □

The above lemma is important since it allows one to reduce the proof that $Q \hookrightarrow H_t$ for some generalized Latin square Q to showing that for every $\sigma : [n] \to \mathbb{F}_r$, Q_σ can be completed to a low-rank matrix.

Definition 16. We say that a two-server private information retrieval scheme $Q \hookrightarrow A$ is *bilinear* if $A = H_t$ for some value of t.

Another way to formulate the above definition is to say that a private information retrieval scheme is bilinear if $\mathscr{U}$ computes the dot product of the servers' answers to obtain the desired value of $\mathbf{x}_i$.

4.3.2 Group-based PIR

Finite groups are a natural source of generalized Latin squares $Q = \mathrm{GLS}[n, T]$. Let $G = \{g_1, \ldots, g_T\}$ be a finite group of size T. Let $S = \{s_1, \ldots, s_n\} \subseteq G$ be an ordered subset of G of size n. A generalized Latin square $Q_{G,S}$ is a $T \times T$ square matrix whose rows and columns are labeled by elements of G, and $Q_{g_1, g_2} = i$ if $g_1 g_2^{-1} = s_i$, while all other locations contain stars.

When a PIR protocol $Q \hookrightarrow A$ uses a generalized Latin square $Q_{G,S}$, we say that this protocol *employs a group-based secret sharing scheme*. Essentially, this means that given an index i, $\mathcal{U}$ maps it to a group element s_i, represents s_i as a random product in the group $s_i = g_1 g_2^{-1}$ and sends g_j to $\mathcal{S}_j$.

The notion of a *group-based* PIR protocol (for which we shall prove a lower bound later) is more restrictive. Let $M \in [r]^{T \times T}$ and let G be a finite group. Assume that the rows and columns of M are labeled by $g_1, \ldots, g_T$. We say that M *respects* G if for every $g_1, g_2, g_3, g_4 \in G$ such that $g_1 g_2^{-1} = g_3 g_4^{-1}$, we have $M_{g_1, g_2} = M_{g_3, g_4}$.

Definition 17. We say that a private information retrieval protocol $Q \hookrightarrow A$ is *group-based* if it employs a secret-sharing scheme based on some group G and for every $\sigma : [n] \to \mathbb{F}_r$ there exists a completion C such that C reduces to A and C respects G.

In other words, a private information retrieval scheme is group-based if the servers represent the database by a function on a finite group G and the scheme allows a user to retrieve the value of this function at any group element using the natural secret-sharing based on G.

4.4 Complexity of bilinear group-based PIR

Consider a bilinear group-based PIR scheme $Q \hookrightarrow H_t$ based on a group G, with answer length t. Clearly, the query length is $\log |G|$. Let $A(r, G, t)$ denote the number of $|G| \times |G|$ matrices over $\mathbb{F}_r$ that respect G (for some fixed labeling $\{g_1, \ldots, g_T\}$ of rows and columns) and have rank at most t. It is easy to see that

$$r^n \leq A(r, G, t), \tag{4.1}$$

since, by Lemma 26, every database yields such a matrix and distinct databases yield distinct matrices. In Subsection 4.4.2, we shall obtain an equivalent algebraic definition for $A(r, G, t)$, and in Subsection 4.4.3, we shall prove an upper bound for $A(r, G, t)$. Our final result is a constraint on the range of possible values of $r, |G|, t$. This constraint implies an $\Omega\left(n^{1/3}\right)$ lower bound for the total communication of any bilinear group-based private information retrieval scheme.

4.4.1 Algebraic preliminaries

Our proof relies on some basic notions of the representation theory of finite groups. The standard references on this subject are [51, 92].

Let $G = \{g_1, \ldots, g_T\}$ be a finite (possibly noncommutative) group. The general linear group $GL_t(\mathbb{F}_r)$ is a multiplicative group of all nondegenerate $t \times t$ matrices over $\mathbb{F}_r$.

- An $\mathbb{F}_r$-*representation* of G of degree t is a homomorphism $\phi : G \to GL_t(\mathbb{F}_r)$.

- A group algebra $\mathbb{F}_r[G]$ of G over a field $\mathbb{F}_r$ is an algebra over $\mathbb{F}_r$ consisting of all possible formal linear combinations

$$\sum_{i=1}^{T} \alpha_i g_i, \quad \{\alpha_i\} \in \mathbb{F}_r.$$

The algebraic operations in $\mathbb{F}_r[G]$ are defined by

$$\sum_i \alpha_i g_i + \sum_i \beta_i g_i = \sum_i (\alpha_i + \beta_i) g_i,$$

$$\left(\sum_i \alpha_i g_i\right) \times \left(\sum_i \beta_i g_i\right) = \sum_{i,j} (\alpha_i \beta_j)(g_i g_j),$$

$$\lambda \left(\sum_i \alpha_i g_i\right) = \sum_i (\lambda \alpha_i) g_i, \quad \lambda \in \mathbb{F}_r.$$

- For an algebra A over $\mathbb{F}_r[G]$, a left A-module is an $\mathbb{F}_r$-linear space on which A acts by left multiplication in such a way that for any $m_1, m_2 \in M$ and any $\alpha, \beta \in \mathbb{F}_r[G]$,

$$\alpha(m_1 + m_2) = \alpha m_1 + \alpha m_2,$$
$$(\alpha + \beta)m_1 = \alpha m_1 + \beta m_1,$$
$$(\alpha\beta)m_1 = \alpha(\beta m_1).$$

The dimension of a module is its dimension as an $\mathbb{F}_r$-linear space. Two A-modules are said to be isomorphic if there exists an isomorphism between them as linear spaces that preserves multiplication by the elements of A.

- There is a one-to-one correspondence between t-dimensional left $\mathbb{F}_r[G]$-modules M, considered up to isomorphism, and $\mathbb{F}_r$-representations of G of degree t, considered up to inner automorphisms of the $GL_t(\mathbb{F}_r)$.

4.4.2 Algebraic formulation

Let $A = \mathbb{F}_r[G]$. For $\alpha \in A$, let $\mathrm{rk}(\alpha) = \dim(A\alpha)$, where $\dim(A\alpha)$ is the dimension of $A\alpha$ as a linear space over $\mathbb{F}_r$. Consider the *regular representation* ϕ of G, $\phi : G \to GL_{|G|}(\mathbb{F}_r)$, defined by

$$(\phi(g))_{g_1, g_2} = \begin{cases} 1, & g_1 g_2^{-1} = g, \\ 0, & \text{otherwise.} \end{cases} \tag{4.2}$$

We extend ϕ to A by linearity. Note that ϕ is an injective algebra homomorphism and that the image of ϕ is the $\mathbb{F}_r$-algebra R of all matrices that respect G. Observe that for any $M \in R$,

$$\mathrm{rk}\, M = \dim\{M'M \mid M' \in R\}. \tag{4.3}$$

To verify (4.3), one needs to note that the first row of a matrix $M' \in R$ can be arbitrary. Therefore the products $M'M$ contain all possible linear combinations of rows of M as their first row. Note also that matrices in R are uniquely determined by their first row. Equation (4.3) follows. It implies an algebraic definition for $A(r, G, t)$:

$$A(r, G, t) = \#\{\alpha \in \mathbb{F}_r[G] \mid \mathrm{rk}(\alpha) \leq t\}. \tag{4.4}$$

4.4.3 Low-dimensional principal ideals in group algebras

Let V be an $\mathbb{F}_r$-linear subspace of A. The left annihilator of V is defined by

$$Ann_L(V) = \{\beta \in A \mid \beta V = 0\}.$$

Similarly, the right annihilator is defined by

$$Ann_R(V) = \{\beta \in A \mid V\beta = 0\}.$$

Clearly, $Ann_L(V)$ is a left ideal in A and $Ann_R(V)$ is a right ideal in A. Let M be a left A-module. The kernel of M is defined by

$$Ker(M) = \{\beta \in A \mid \beta M = 0\}.$$

It is straightforward to verify that $Ker(M)$ is a two-sided ideal that coincides with $Ann_L(M)$ if M is a left ideal in A.

Lemma 27. *The number of t-dimensional left A-modules counted up to isomorphism is at most $r^{\log|G|t^2}$.*

Proof. The fourth item in the bullet list in Subsection 4.4.1 implies that it suffices to count $\mathbb{F}_r$-representations of G of degree t. Let $g_1, \ldots, g_s$ be the set of generators of G, where $s \leq \log|G|$. Now we have only to note that every representation $\phi : G \to GL_t(\mathbb{F}_r)$ is uniquely specified by s matrices $\phi(g_1), \ldots, \phi(g_s)$, each of size $t \times t$. □

Clearly, isomorphic modules have identical kernels. Now we show that the kernel of a low-dimensional module has a high dimension.

Lemma 28. *Let M be a t-dimensional left A-module; then the dimension of $Ker(M)$ as an $\mathbb{F}_r$-linear space is at least $|G| - t^2$.*

Proof. Note that multiplication by an element of A induces a linear transformation of M. Such a transformation can be expressed by a $t \times t$ matrix. Multiplication by a linear combination of elements of A corresponds a to linear combination of the corresponding matrices. Therefore we conclude that $\dim Ker(M) \geq |G| - t^2$. □

Lemma 29. *Suppose that V is an $\mathbb{F}_r$-linear subspace of A; then*

$$\dim(Ann_R(V)) \leq |G| - \dim(V).$$

Proof. Consider a bilinear map $l : A \otimes A \to \mathbb{F}_r$, setting $l(x \otimes y)$ equal to the coefficient of 1 in the expansion of xy in the group basis. Clearly, l has full rank (since, in the group basis, l is defined by an identity matrix up to a permutation of columns). However, $l(V \otimes Ann_R(V)) = 0$. Thus $\dim(Ann_R(V)) \leq |G| - \dim(V)$. $\qquad \square$

Our main technical result is given by the following theorem.

Theorem 22. *For arbitrary finite group G and arbitrary values of r and t,*

$$A(r,G,t) \leq r^{O(\log |G| t^2)}.$$

Proof. Let $\alpha \in A$ be such that $\mathrm{rk}(\alpha) \leq t$. Consider $A\alpha$ as a left A-module. Observe that $Ker(A\alpha)$ is a two-sided ideal $I = Ann_L(A\alpha)$. Note that $\alpha \in Ann_R(I)$. By Lemma 27, every A-module of dimension up to t has a kernel that belongs to a family of at most $tr^{\log |G| t^2}$ ideals. Also, by Lemmas 28 and 29, there are at most r^{t^2} elements in $Ann_R(I)$ for every I. $\qquad \square$

Combining (4.1) with Theorem 22, we obtain our main result.

Theorem 23. *Let $Q \hookrightarrow H_t$ be a bilinear group-based PIR scheme over a group G. Let $q = \log |G|$ denote the query length and let t denote the answer length; then*

$$n \leq O\left(qt^2\right).$$

In particular, the total communication of any such scheme is $\Omega\left(n^{1/3}\right)$.

4.5 Summary of lower bounds for two-server PIR

In Sections 4.3 and 4.4, we introduced a new, though quite natural combinatorial view of the two-server PIR problem, and obtained a lower bound for the communication complexity of PIR in a restricted (bilinear group-based) model that captures all currently known PIR protocols [76, appendix]. Stated informally, our main result is that if the servers represent the database by a function on a finite group, if the protocol allows the user to retrieve the value of this function at any group element, and if the user computes the dot product of the responses of the servers to obtain the final answer, the communication complexity has to be $\Omega\left(n^{1/3}\right)$.

Clearly, our lower bound admits two interpretations. On the one hand, it can be viewed as a witness in support of the conjecture of Chor et al. [28] that their PIR protocol with $O\left(n^{1/3}\right)$ communication is asymptotically optimal. On the other hand, our result demonstrates a common shortcoming of the existing upper-bound techniques and thus, hopefully, may provide some directions for future work on upper bounds.

4.6 Addendum

Our constructions of private information retrieval schemes in this chapter follow via a direct reduction from locally decodable codes. In the last few years constructions of LDCs have been substantially improved [20, 36, 38, 55]. (See Section 3.7 for a detailed discussion of the improvements.) Improved constructions of LDCs yield improved constructions of private information retrieval schemes.

Specifically, the results of Efremenko [38] yield a family of 2^t-server private information retrieval schemes with $\exp\left((\log n)^{1/t}(\log\log n)^{1-1/t}\right)$ communication to access an n-bit database for every $t \geq 2$. See also [55].

References

1. Great Internet Mersenne Prime search, June 2010. http://www.mersenne.org/.
2. Lenstra–Pomerance–Wagstaff conjecture, June 2010. In Wikipedia. The Free Encyclopedia, http://en.wikipedia.org/wiki/Main_Page.
3. The Prime Pages, June 2010. http://primes.utm.edu/.
4. Martin Abadi, Joan Feigenbaum, and Joe Kilian. On hiding information from an oracle. *Journal of Computer and System Sciences*, 39:21–50, 1989.
5. Manindra Agrawal, Neeraj Kayal, and Nitin Saxena. PRIMES is in P. *Annals of Mathematics*, 160:781–793, 2004.
6. Andris Ambainis. Upper bound on the communication complexity of private information retrieval. In *32nd International Colloquium on Automata, Languages and Programming (ICALP)*, volume 1256 of Lecture Notes in Computer Science, pages 401–407. Springer, Berlin, Heidelberg, 1997.
7. Laszlo Babai, Lance Fortnow, Leonid Levin, and Mario Szegedy. Checking computations in polylogarithmic time. In *23rd ACM Symposium on Theory of Computing (STOC)*, pages 21–31, 1991.
8. Laszlo Babai, Lance Fortnow, Naom Nisan, and Avi Wigderson. BPP has subexponential time simulations unless EXPTIME has publishable proofs. *Computational Complexity*, 3:307–318, 1993.
9. Omer Barkol, Yuval Ishai, and Enav Weinreb. On locally decodable codes, self-correctable codes, and t-private PIR. In *International Workshop on Randomization and Computation (RANDOM)*, pages 311–325, 2007.
10. Donald Beaver and Joan Feigenbaum. Hiding instances in multioracle queries. In *7th International Symposium on Theoretical Aspects of Computer Science (STACS)*, volume 415 of Lecture Notes in Computer Science, pages 37–48. Springer, Berlin, Heidelberg, 1990.
11. Donald Beaver, Joan Feigenbaum, Joe Kilian, and Phillip Rogaway. Security with low communication overhead. In *International Cryptology Conference (CRYPTO)*, pages 62–76, 1990.
12. Donald Beaver, Silvio Micali, and Pillip Rogaway. The round complexity of secure protocols. In *22nd ACM Symposium on Theory of Computing (STOC)*, pages 503–513, 1990.
13. Edwin Beckenbach and Richard Bellman. *Inequalities*. Springer-Verlag, Berlin, 1965.
14. Richard Beigel, Lance Fortnow, and William Gasarch. A tight lower bound for restricted PIR protocols. *Computational Complexity*, 15:82–91, 2006.
15. Amos Beimel, Yuval Ishai, and Eyal Kushilevitz. General constructions for information-theoretic private information retrieval. *Journal of Computer and System Sciences*, 71:213–247, 2005.
16. Amos Beimel, Yuval Ishai, Eyal Kushilevitz, and Tal Malkin. One-way functions are essential for single-server private information retrieval. In *31st ACM Symposium on Theory of Computing (STOC)*, pages 89–98, 1999.

17. Amos Beimel, Yuval Ishai, Eyal Kushilevitz, and Jean-Francios Raymond. Breaking the $O\left(n^{1/(2k-1)}\right)$ barrier for information-theoretic private information retrieval. In *43rd IEEE Symposium on Foundations of Computer Science (FOCS)*, pages 261–270, 2002.
18. Amos Beimel, Yuval Ishai, and Tal Malkin. Reducing the servers' computation in private information retrieval: PIR with preprocessing. In *International Cryptology Conference (CRYPTO)*, volume 1880 of Lecture Notes in Computer Science, pages 56–74. Springer, Berlin, Heidelberg, 2000.
19. Amos Beimel and Yoav Stahl. Robust information theoretic private information retrieval. In *3rd Conference on Security in Communication Networks*, 2002.
20. Avraham Ben-Aroya, Klim Efremenko, and Amnon Ta-Shma. Local list decoding with a constant number of queries. In *51st IEEE Symposium on Foundations of Computer Science (FOCS)*, 2010. to appear.
21. Michael Ben-Or, Shafi Goldwasser, and Avi Wigderson. Completeness theorems for non-cryptographic fault-tolerant distributed computation. In *20th ACM Symposium on Theory of Computing (STOC)*, pages 1–10, 1988.
22. Manuel Blum, Michael Luby, and Ronitt Rubinfeld. Self-testing/correcting with applications to numerical problems. *Journal of Computer and System Sciences*, 47:549–595, 1993.
23. Jean Bourgain and Mei-Chu Chang. A Gauss sum estimate in arbitrary finite fields. *Comptes Rendus Mathematique*, 342:643–646, 2006.
24. Christian Cachin, Silvio Micali, and Markus Stadler. Computationally private information retrieval with polylogarithmic communication. In *International Cryptology Conference (EUROCRYPT)*, volume 1592 of Lecture Notes in Computer Science, pages 402–414. Springer, Berlin, Heidelberg, 1999.
25. Ran Canetti, Yuval Ishai, Ravi Kumar, Michael Reiter, Ronitt Rubinfeld, and Rebecca Wright. Selective private function evaluation with applications to private statistics. In *20th ACM Symposium on Principles of Distributed Computing (PODC)*, pages 293–304, 2001.
26. David Chaum, Claude Crepeau, and Ivan Damgard. Multiparty unconditionally secure protocols. In *20th ACM Symposium on Theory of Computing (STOC)*, pages 11–19, 1988.
27. Victor Chen, Elena Grigorescu, and Ronald de Wolf. Efficient and error-correcting data structures for membership and polynomial evaluation. In *27th Symposium on Theoretical Aspects of Computer Science (STACS)*, 2010.
28. Benny Chor, Oded Goldreich, Eyal Kushilevitz, and Madhu Sudan. Private information retrieval. *Journal of the ACM*, 45:965–981, 1998.
29. David Cox, John Little, and Donal O'Shea. *Ideals, Varieties, and Algorithms: An Introduction to Computational Algebraic Geometry and Commutative Algebra*. Springer, New York, 1996.
30. Ronald de Wolf. Error-correcting data structures. In *26th Annual Symposium on Theoretical Aspects of Computer Science (STACS 09)*, pages 313–324, 2009.
31. B.L. Van der Waerden. *Algebra*. Springer, Berlin, Heidelberg, 2003.
32. A. Deshpande, R. Jain, T. Kavitha, S. Lokam, and J. Radhakrishnan. Better lower bounds for locally decodable codes. In *20th IEEE Computational Complexity Conference (CCC)*, pages 184–193, 2002.
33. Giovanni Di-Crescenzo, Yuval Ishai, and Rafail Ostrovsky. Universal service-providers for private information retrieval. *Journal of Cryptology*, 14:37–74, 2001.
34. Giovanni Di-Crescenzo, Tal Malkin, and Rafail Ostrovsky. Single-database private information retrieval implies oblivious transfer. In *International Cryptology Conference (EUROCRYPT)*, volume 1807 of Lecture Notes in Computer Science, pages 122–138. Springer, Berlin, Heidelberg, 2000.
35. Zeev Dvir. On matrix rigidity and locally self-correctable codes. In *26th IEEE Computational Complexity Conference (CCC)*, pages 102–113, 2010.
36. Zeev Dvir, Parikshit Gopalan, and Sergey Yekhanin. Matching vector codes. In *51st IEEE Symposium on Foundations of Computer Science (FOCS)*, 2010. to appear.
37. Zeev Dvir and Amir Shpilka. Locally decodable codes with 2 queries and polynomial identity testing for depth 3 circuits. *SIAM Journal on Computing*, 36(5):1404–1434, 2006.

38. Klim Efremenko. 3-query locally decodable codes of subexponential length. In *41st ACM Symposium on Theory of Computing (STOC)*, pages 39–44, 2009.
39. Paul Erdös and T. N. Shorey. On the greatest prime factor of $2^p - 1$ for a prime p and other expressions. *Acta Arithmetica*, 30:257–265, 1976.
40. Eldar Fischer, Eric Lehman, Ilan Newman, Sofya Raskhodinkova, Ronitt Rubinfeld, and Alex Samorodnitsky. Monotonicity testing over the general poset domains. In *34th ACM Symposium on Theory of Computing (STOC)*, pages 474–483, 2002.
41. Kevin Ford, Florian Luca, and Igor Shparlinski. On the largest prime factor of the Mersenne numbers. *Bulletin of the Australian Mathematical Society*, 79:455–463, 2009.
42. Anna Gal and Andrew Mills. Three query locally decodable codes with higher correctness require exponential length. Manuscript, submitted, 2009.
43. William Gasarch. A survey on private information retrieval. *The Bulletin of the EATCS*, 82:72–107, 2004.
44. Craig Gentry and Zulfikar Ramzan. Single-database private information retrieval with constant communication rate. In *32nd International Colloquium on Automata, Languages and Programming (ICALP)*, pages 803–815, 2005.
45. Yael Gertner, Shafi Goldwasser, and Tal Malkin. A random server model for private information retrieval. In *International Workshop on Randomization and Computation (RANDOM)*, volume 1518 of Lecture Notes in Computer Science, pages 200–217. Springer, Berlin, Heidelberg, 1998.
46. Yael Gertner, Yuval Ishai, Eyal Kushilevitz, and Tal Malkin. Protecting data privacy in private information retrieval schemes. *Journal of Computer and System Sciences*, 60:592–629, 2000.
47. Oded Goldreich. Short locally testable codes and proofs. In *Electronic Colloquium on Computational Complexity (ECCC)*, TR05-014, 2005.
48. Oded Goldreich, Howard Karloff, Leonard Schulman, and Luca Trevisan. Lower bounds for locally decodable codes and private information retrieval. In *17th IEEE Computational Complexity Conference (CCC)*, pages 175–183, 2002.
49. Vince Grolmusz. Superpolynomial size set-systems with restricted intersections mod 6 and explicit Ramsey graphs. *Combinatorica*, 20:71–86, 2000.
50. Vince Grolmusz. Constructing set-systems with prescribed intersection sizes. *Journal of Algorithms*, 44:321–337, 2002.
51. I. Martin Isaacs. *Character Theory of Finite Groups*. AMS Chelsea Publishing, Providence, Rhode Island, 1976.
52. Yuval Ishai and Eyal Kushilevitz. On the hardness of information-theoretic multiparty computation. In *Eurocrypt 2004*, volume 3027 of Lecture Notes in Computer Science, pages 439–455. Springer, Berlin, Heidelberg, 2004.
53. Toshiya Itoh. Efficient private information retrieval. *IEICE Transactions on the Fundamentals of Electronics, Communication and Computer Science*, E82-A:11–20, 1999.
54. Toshiya Itoh. On lower bounds for the communication complexity of private information retrieval. *IEICE Transactions on the Fundamentals of Electronics, Communication and Computer Science*, pages 157–164, 2001.
55. Toshiya Itoh and Yasuhiro Suzuki. New constructions for query-efficient locally decodable codes of subexponential length. *IEICE Transactions on Information and Systems*, pages 263–270, 2010.
56. Jonathan Katz and Luca Trevisan. On the efficiency of local decoding procedures for error-correcting codes. In *32nd ACM Symposium on Theory of Computing (STOC)*, pages 80–86, 2000.
57. Kiran S. Kedlaya and Sergey Yekhanin. Locally decodable codes from nice subsets of finite fields and prime factors of Mersenne numbers. *SIAM Journal on Computing*, 38:1952–1969, 2009.
58. Iordanis Kerenidis and Ronald de Wolf. Exponential lower bound for 2-query locally decodable codes via a quantum argument. *Journal of Computer and System Sciences*, 69:395–420, 2004.

59. Aggelos Kiayias and Moti Yung. Secure games with polynomial expressions. In *28th International Colloquium on Automata, Languages and Programming (ICALP)*, volume 2076 of Lecture Notes in Computer Science, pages 939–950. Springer, Berlin, Heidelberg, 2001.

60. Eyal Kushilevitz and Rafail Ostrovsky. Replication is not needed: Single-database computationally-private information retrieval. In *38rd IEEE Symposium on Foundations of Computer Science (FOCS)*, pages 364–373, 1997.

61. Eyal Kushilevitz and Rafail Ostrovsky. One-way trapdoor permutations are sufficient for single-database computationally-private information retrieval. In *International Cryptology Conference (EUROCRYPT)*, volume 1807 of Lecture Notes in Computer Science, pages 104–121. Springer, Berlin, Heidelberg, 2000.

62. Rudolf Lidl and Harald Niederreiter. *Finite Fields*. Cambridge University Press, Cambridge, 1983.

63. Helger Lipmaa. An oblivious transfer protocol with log-squared communication. International Association for Cryptologic Research, Technical Report 2004/063, 2004.

64. Richard Lipton. Efficient checking of computations. In *7th International Symposium on Theoretical Aspects of Computer Science (STACS)*, volume 415 of Lecture Notes in Computer Science, pages 207–215. Springer, Berlin, Heidelberg, 1990.

65. F. J. MacWilliams and N. J. A. Sloane. *The Theory of Error Correcting Codes*. North Holland, Amsterdam, New York.

66. Eran Mann. Private access to distributed information. Master's thesis, Technion, Israel Institute of Technology, Haifa, 1998.

67. Leo Murata and Carl Pomerance. On the largest prime factor of a Mersenne number. *Number theory, CRM Proceedings, Lecture Notes of the American Mathematical Society*, 36:209–218, 2004.

68. M. Murty and S. Wong. The ABC conjecture and prime divisors of the Lucas and Lehmer sequences. In *Millennial Conference on Number Theory III*, pages 43–54, Urbana, IL, 2000.

69. Moni Naor and Benny Pinkas. Oblivious transfer and polynomial evaluation. In *29th ACM Symposium on Theory of Computing (STOC)*, pages 245–254, 1999.

70. Kenji Obata. Optimal lower bounds for 2-query locally decodable linear codes. In *6th International Workshop on Randomization and Computation (RANDOM)*, volume 2483 of Lecture Notes in Computer Science, pages 39–50. Springer, Berlin, Heidelberg, 2002.

71. Rafail Ostrovsky and Victor Shoup. Private information storage. In *29th ACM Symposium on Theory of Computing (STOC)*, pages 294–303, 1997.

72. Rafail Ostrovsky and William Skeith. A survey of single database PIR: techniques and applications. In *10th International Conference on Practice and Theory in Public-Key Cryptography (PKC)*, pages 393–411, 2007.

73. Alexander Polishchuk and Daniel Spielman. Nearly-linear size holographic proofs. In *26th ACM Symposium on Theory of Computing (STOC)*, pages 194–203, 1994.

74. Carl Pomerance. Recent developments in primality testing. *Mathematical Intelligencer*, 3:97–105, 1980.

75. Prasad Raghavendra. A note on Yekhanin's locally decodable codes. In *Electronic Colloquium on Computational Complexity (ECCC)*, TR07-016, 2007.

76. Alexander Razborov and Sergey Yekhanin. An $\Omega(n^{1/3})$ lower bound for bilinear group based private information retrieval. *Theory of Computing*, 3:221–238, 2007.

77. Andrei Romashchenko. Reliable computations based on locally decodable codes. In *23rd International Symposium on Theoretical Aspects of Computer Science (STACS)*, volume 3884 of Lecture Notes in Computer Science, pages 537–548. Springer, Berlin, Heidelberg, 2006.

78. M. Rosen. A proof of the Lucas–Lehmer test. *American Mathematical Monthly*, 95:855–856, 1988.

79. Imre Ruzsa and Endre Szemeredi. Triple systems with no six points carrying three triangles. *Colloquia Mathematica Societatis Janos Bolyai*, 18:939–945, 1978.

80. Gabor Sarkozy and Stanley Selkow. An extension to the Ruzsa–Szemeredi theorem. *Combinatorica*, 25:77–84, 2005.

81. Peter Sarnak, 2007. Personal communication.

82. A. Schinzel. On primitive factors of $a^n - b^n$. *Proceedings of the Cambridge Philosophical Society*, 58:555–562, 1962.
83. Julien Stern. A new and efficient all-or-nothing disclosure of secrets protocol. In *International Cryptology Conference (ASIACRYPT)*, volume 1514 of Lecture Notes in Computer Science, pages 357–371. Springer, Berlin, Heidelberg, 1998.
84. C. Stewart. The greatest prime factor of $a^n - b^n$. *Acta Arithmetica*, 26:427–433, 1974.
85. C. Stewart. On divisors of Fermat, Fibonacci, Lucas, and Lehmer numbers. *Proceedings of the London Mathematical Society*, 35:425–447, 1977.
86. Madhu Sudan. *Efficient checking of polynomials and proofs and the hardness of approximation problems*. PhD thesis, University of California at Berkeley, 1992.
87. Madhu Sudan, Luca Trevisan, and Salil Vadhan. Pseudorandom generators without the XOR lemma. In *39th ACM Symposium on Theory of Computing (STOC)*, pages 537–546, 1999.
88. Luca Trevisan. Some applications of coding theory in computational complexity. *Quaderni di Matematica*, 13:347–424, 2004.
89. J.H. van Lint. *Introduction to Coding Theory*. Springer-Verlag, Berlin, Heidelberg, 1982.
90. Samuel Wagstaff. Divisors of Mersenne numbers. *Mathematics of Computation*, 40:385–397, 1983.
91. Stephanie Wehner and Ronald de Wolf. Improved lower bounds for locally decodable codes and private information retrieval. In *32nd International Colloquium on Automata, Languages and Programming (ICALP)*, volume 3580 of Lecture Notes in Computer Science, pages 1424–1436. Springer, Berlin, Heidelberg, 2005.
92. S.H. Weintraub. *Representation Theory of Finite Groups: Algebra and Arithmetic*. Graduate Studies in Mathematics. American Mathematical Society, Providence, RI, 2003.
93. David Woodruff. New lower bounds for general locally decodable codes. In *Electronic Colloquium on Computational Complexity (ECCC)*, TR07-006, 2007.
94. David Woodruff. Corruption and recovery-efficient locally decodable codes. In *International Workshop on Randomization and Computation (RANDOM)*, pages 584–595, 2008.
95. David Woodruff and Sergey Yekhanin. A geometric approach to information theoretic private information retrieval. In *20th IEEE Computational Complexity Conference (CCC)*, pages 275–284, 2005.
96. Sergey Yekhanin. New locally decodable codes and private information retrieval schemes. In *Electronic Colloquium on Computational Complexity (ECCC)*, TR06-127, 2006.
97. Sergey Yekhanin. Towards 3-query locally decodable codes of subexponential length. *Journal of the ACM*, 55:1–16, 2008.
98. Sergey Yekhanin. Private information retrieval. *Communications of the ACM*, 53(4):68–73, 2010.

Index